# MR. BUSH'S
# WAR

# MR. BUSH'S WAR

## Adventures in the Politics of Illusion

# STEPHEN R. GRAUBARD

HILL and WANG
*A division of Farrar, Straus and Giroux*
NEW YORK

*Copyright © 1992 by Stephen R. Graubard*

ALL RIGHTS RESERVED

*Printed in the United States of America*

*Published simultaneously in Canada by HarperCollinsCanadaLtd*

DESIGNED BY TERE LO PRETE

*First edition, 1992*

Library of Congress Cataloging-in-Publication Data
Graubard, Stephen Richards.
   Mr. Bush's war : adventures in the politics of illusion / Stephen R.
Graubard. — 1st ed.
     p.   cm.
   1. Bush, George, 1924–    . 2. Persian Gulf War, 1991.
I. Title.  II. Title: Mister Bush's war.
   E882.2.G73  1991    973.928—dc20     91-12202    CIP

*For a New Generation*

# Contents

# Preface

This book had its beginnings in London, in those long, torrid early August days when Iraq invaded and occupied Kuwait and the British Prime Minister, appearing at a news conference with the American President in Colorado, heard Mr. Bush describe the Iraqi action as one of "naked aggression." Both spoke of the possibility of economic or even military action under United Nations auspices. That their response was so vigorous suggested that something even more important than the defense of international law or the protection of a vital economic interest—access to Middle Eastern oil at a reasonable price—was at stake. Given the President's lackluster performance in his first eighteen months in office, with substantial economic and social problems perpetually confronting him, the Iraqi invasion must have seemed an almost welcome diversion from intractable domestic concerns.

Eight years of loyal and silent service in the Reagan administration had taught the President many things, not least about Margaret Thatcher. Her boldness in confronting Argentinian aggression in the Falklands had given her new stature at home and great repute abroad. More importantly, at least for the

President, who never failed to consult the polls, it guaranteed her a second term at Number 10 Downing Street. Her reputation assured as a woman of courage and principle, she emerged from the Falklands ordeal with an aura of infallibility that she never wholly lost.

Was the Falklands campaign replicable on a larger and more conspicuous world stage, giving comparable advantages to the United States and its bold President? While Iraq's leader, Saddam Hussein, a major Soviet client in the Middle East, boasted a military capability far greater than what Argentina's Leopoldo Galtieri claimed in 1982, decisive British actions nevertheless had rapidly annulled any initial advantage that the aggressor enjoyed. Margaret Thatcher, knowing that no one would intervene to help Argentina, achieved her victory at small cost and, allowing for the distances, in record time. The extent of her influence on the President's subsequent actions is difficult to establish, but certainly her success in winning a "splendid little war" and the effect this had on her future political career cannot have been lost on the President.

Without the Secretary of State at his side—indeed, with no major American adviser in attendance—he took a decision of great importance that carried almost no risk. He, a child of the 1930s, would never appease an aggressive dictator; the Iraqi invasion of Kuwait would not be allowed to stand. Saddam Hussein would either withdraw his armies, obeying the resolutions quickly passed by the United Nations Security Council, or confront severe economic hardship, perhaps chaos, created by a system of strict international sanctions. Meanwhile, a hastily assembled American military force, rapidly dispatched, stood ready to defend Saudi Arabia. The President, recognizing very early that, whatever the outcome, he could not himself lose, took the position Mrs. Thatcher had taken a decade earlier at substantially greater political risk to herself.

Bush knew that if Saddam Hussein withdrew, as Galtieri had not done, the victory would be his; if, foolishly, Saddam chose not to withdraw and a military campaign was required to dislodge him from Kuwait, the American forces would win easily, as the British had in the Falklands. The President, knowing Mrs. Thatcher, was certain of British military assistance to reciprocate the discreet American assistance given in the Falklands war. And, more importantly, he could be confident that the Soviet Union, preoccupied with almost insuperable domestic problems, would not risk intervention despite its long-standing friendship with Iraq.

The decision to condemn the invasion of Kuwait and mobilize American forces for rapid deployment in the Gulf was hazard-free. The art of politics required the President to pretend otherwise. Unless the operation was considered to be fraught with peril, the American victory, when it came, would be devalued, discounted as a minor affair. So it came to be that the President, as portrayed by his friends, took on the qualities of a latter-day Winston Churchill; in his own vivid imagination, and in his halting inarticulateness, he consciously assumed the role: he was risking all, including that most precious thing, his reelection, to resist aggression, to do what the European democracies had failed to do in the 1930s, to their ultimate shame and ruin. Bush's appropriation of Churchill's mantle was a calculated political strategy.

Some Democrat in Congress ought to have laughed at the mask, seen it for what it was; someone in the large press and television news corps ought to have recognized its incongruity. These failures revealed how few had learned the truth about George Bush, the political son and chosen heir of Ronald Reagan. Though Hollywood figured not at all in his background—he was a Texas oilman, at least in his own perception—Bush had learned a great deal from watching an actor perform at the White House. To pretend to be Winston Churchill, making Saddam Hussein out to be Adolf Hitler, was to spin a fable worthy of the master himself. Someone ought to have ridiculed the effort in its first days. It wildly exaggerated the qualities of Saddam; it wholly robbed Churchill of his true distinction. The idea that the President, a man who had never once in the past resisted the Iraqi dictator, could from one day to the next make him democracy's principal foe was itself a caricature of what Churchill had done. Bush had never recognized the Iraqi dictator for what he was; in eight years as Vice President and eighteen months as President, he had never warned the nation against him. Indeed, he never understood him. How could he have done so when he knew so little about the Middle East or elsewhere?

Is it possible that a later generation, looking at the Reagan-Bush era, will choose so to characterize it, mocking its "splendid little wars" against inconsequential foes, magnified to appear so much greater than they were? These military actions produced satisfaction at home; they gave the illusion of decisive action by men unwilling to abide dictators, whether in Grenada, Libya, Panama, or Iraq. They replicated, in fictional form, the tragedies and dramas of the 1930s; they deflected the nation's attention from the crises and opportunities of the 1980s and 1990s. For President Bush, like his predecessor, knew little of the world and was so abysmally ignorant of its complexities as to genuinely mistake a temporary political gain for himself and his party for a national and international gain, and to herald it as such.

The plea of that small minority who questioned the President's policy of sending troops to the Gulf—"no war for oil" —was followed a few months later by a more insistent demand, especially in Congress, to "give sanctions a chance." Both passionate sentiments wholly misconceived the political situation of the day; they failed to understand either the mind or the intentions of the President. They took into account none of his memories or experiences as a politician.

The news media did much to befog the atmosphere still further, defining the issues either as the White House framed them for the press or as they imagined them. The breathless

commentator who, in his habitual excited, noisy Sunday manner, like so many others of his ilk, warned of the body bags
that would soon descend on the country, spoke in an idiom
that reflected a mind-set shaped wholly by the events of
America's Vietnam experience and not of something so insignificant as Thatcher's Falklands war. Reflecting constantly on
Lyndon Johnson when they would have done better to dwell
on Ronald Reagan and his loyal disciple, George Bush, they
missed the only story worth telling.

Those American journalists and politicians of a certain
generation, galloping through middle age, said to have been
"traumatized" by Vietnam, failed to see the difference between
jungle and desert, between a foe constantly resupplied and
one that had no access to new supplies, between a guerrilla
operation and one that put the Iraqi Army, including its
vaunted Republican Guards, in fixed positions, an extended
poor man's Maginot Line, waiting to be cracked from the air
by the most modern weapons. Am I saying that the President
acted principally out of a concern with himself, with his own
political future and that of the Republican Party? Yes. There
is no doubt that the President knew what he wanted as early
as August 2. If Saddam retreated and left Kuwait, the President
would win politically; if Saddam resisted and remained in
Kuwait, the President would win politically and militarily. He
would prove himself a risk taker, a man faithful to his word.

The political genius of the President lay in his insistence that
it was all going to be hard, exceedingly dangerous, but that he
would persevere and win in the end. The truth was that it
would be all relatively easy, and had to be, given the differences
between the military equipment and the potential of the two
adversaries. What made it a *drôle de guerre*—a phony war—was
precisely that nothing was asked of anyone except those
hundreds of thousands of men and women actually sent to
serve in the Gulf. For a while, it even looked like the war would
cost nothing, or almost nothing; members of the Bush admin-

istration's Coalition would, it was hoped, pay most of the
expenses of the war. A great effort was made to insist that
the Americans had not become the paid "mercenaries" of the
Saudis, even if the Saudis had emerged as paymaster in chief.
In any case, all this was secondary to a larger presidential
purpose; in mobilizing the nation behind him, the President
allowed the Congress to cavil and rail, even to seem for a
moment to threaten the execution of his well-laid military
plans. The President knew these to be harmless diversions;
recalcitrant members of Congress, to be tarred by the brush
of nonpatriotism, would no more prevail than those faint-
hearted MPs who had thought to thwart Margaret Thatcher.

George Bush is a man of World War II, yet he never really
understood the world created by that war or by the Cold War
that followed. Familiar with some of the policy landmarks of
the Cold War, insofar as they reflected American-Soviet rivalry,
he knew not at all what to do when the terrain of American-
Soviet competition in its old form disappeared. A person whose
Republican sympathies and narrow experience of life never
allowed him to understand even Franklin Roosevelt—as Ronald
Reagan, in his own more Depression-influenced early adulthood did—George Bush lived with the romantic and idealized
Hollywood representations of war. And like so many other
Americans, both Republican and Democratic, his World War
II hero was Churchill, the man who stood up to Hitler and
never appeased him. For an American to admire Churchill,
even if one did not wholly agree with all his policies, particularly
in respect to the Empire, was to take an absolutely safe position.
It brought you into conflict with no one. Yet, in the way the
President used the Churchill story, pretending that it had some
reference to himself, he showed political skill, electoral greed,
and intellectual dishonesty.

A statesman who makes war needs to think always of the
peace that will follow. In this, as in so much else, President
Bush showed himself a rank amateur. He knew neither when

to stop the war nor how to conduct it so as to achieve larger and more morally defensible ends. His great concern, taught him by his own very limited experience, was to avoid the hazard of American soldiers being killed in the streets of Baghdad, as 241 American Marines had been killed in 1983 in their Beirut barracks. The President had no idea of what sort of settlement could be made in the Middle East; his Secretary of State, equally innocent, imagined that he could push the Israelis to come to the negotiating table, finally restoring land to Arabs in return for diplomatic recognition: the Coalition pressure for them to do so would be irresistible. Both the President and the Secretary vastly exaggerated their own powers. Worse, they greatly underestimated the complexities of the Middle East, where Iran was arguably as consequential as Israel and where inter-Arab and inter-Muslim rivalry was intense, creating and dissolving alliances, where nationalist, religious, and ethnic violence was scarcely less endemic than in many other parts of the world, including the Soviet Union, Europe, Asia, and Africa.

There was, however, a greater failure. The Gulf War was a "nothing war"; it resolved nothing and settled nothing. Another war, however, and a far more real one, was indeed ending; two Presidents, of the United States and the Soviet Union, insisted that the Cold War was finally over. Did President Bush believe what he said? Did he understand what options it created for him? Did he and those few who huddled about him, talking about hardball, softball, and pinball—of throwing fast curves, slow pitches, "tilting" now one way, then another—have any notion of the character of the post-Cold War world they talked about? Could men so deficient in their knowledge of history, including that of the twentieth century, be capable of making a just and lasting peace? Would they know how to start on such a vast effort, realizing that it could no longer be guided by the limited objectives first sketched out in the Nixon years, when the President served as the United States Ambassador to the United Nations?

This book—my interpretation of the Gulf War, Mr. Bush's war—owes a great deal to both Winston Churchill and John Maynard Keynes. Their books led me to embark on researches I might not otherwise have considered, reflecting on war and peace as I might not otherwise have done. More importantly, their books helped me understand why passion is a necessary ingredient for a writer who wishes to comment with any degree of candor on the tragic century in which we live. The book's dedication, "For a New Generation," allows me to thank my sons, William and David, who helped me in more ways than they know, who happily belong to that new generation. It also allows me to say that my wife, Margaret, has been my principal guide and critic; she has saved me from accepting too easily the explanations of those who show too little concern for fair play, the art of the civilized. My purpose has not been to find fault only with Presidents; it is, rather, to grieve over a nation that is today being infantilized, that has lost its way, that must seek again to find it, for others' as well as for its own sake.

# MR. BUSH'S
# WAR

# The Political
# Strategy

President Bush, from the first days of August, wrapped himself in the mantle of Winston Churchill, wishing to appear as the American leader who would have no truck with dictators. It was an artful disguise, calculated to produce large political advantages. The idea of comparing himself publicly with Prime Minister Thatcher, proposing to stop Iraqi aggression as she had halted Argentina's invasion of the Falklands a decade earlier, had no appeal for the President. Mrs. Thatcher's actions scarcely vibrated for the American public; Churchill, on the other hand, for Americans as for the rest of the world, was a mythic figure who never compromised with a mighty foe, bringing Hitler and his detestable regime down to ignominious defeat. To be compared with such a man was to realize all one's fantasies, achieving the kind of political status no one would think to question or disparage.

The President's words, implicitly if not explicitly, invited such comparison. The political scenario mounted by the Bush administration required Iraq to be the equivalent of the Nazi German rogue state, Saddam Hussein the new Hitler, and Bush the valiant appeasement-resisting Churchill. Modesty required the last to be said sotto voce, but Bush, in his few public utterances, referred constantly to "blitzkrieg," Munich, and a lying dictator who had deceived the world as Hitler had once deceived Europe. And so Saddam was converted into an Arab Hitler; Iraq, a miserable country that made vast purchases of modern arms with its abundant oil revenues, was made to resemble the Nazi Germany of the 1930s. The fact that Saddam never enjoyed the victories that came to Hitler so effortlessly in the 1930s when, through political chicanery and diplomatic skill, he absorbed two sovereign and independent states, Austria and Czechoslovakia, was a detail scarcely ever mentioned. Indeed, the Iraqi invasion of an Islamic state, Iran, which had led to a destructive eight-year war that ended inconclusively, was equally ignored. Saddam had never achieved military successes comparable to Hitler's; there was nothing vaguely resembling the Nazi "blitzkrieg," forcing states thought to be as militarily powerful as Poland and France to capitulate in a matter of weeks. Still, Iraq's supply of chemical weapons, already used, and its reputed biological weapons capability, not to speak of its air force and Republican Guards, made him seem the commander of a frightening military force.

It was a superb political argument, admirably crafted. The possibility that the President believed it cannot be wholly discounted. The disguise, the playacting, was magnificent political theater, but it had little to do with reality. That no one saw the "appeasement" theme for what it was—a conventional political ploy calculated principally to achieve an electoral victory for the President in 1992—suggested the damage done to the American political process by an even more accomplished and brazen theatrical performance, that of George Bush's teacher and mentor, Ronald Reagan.

Winston Churchill, in suggesting that there had never been "a war more easy to stop than that which has just wrecked what has been left of the world from the previous struggle," spoke of World War II in a way that President Bush could never speak of Iraq's invasion of Kuwait or what he and his Coalition partners planned to do if Saddam did not pull out before January 15. The reason, quite simply, was that the President and many of his allies were themselves responsible for creating Saddam, arming him, allowing him to murder Kurds, Iraqis, Iranians, and others for more than a decade. Churchill, in faulting a whole generation of democratic political leaders, and not only in the United Kingdom, but also in France and the United States, avoided the easy temptation to attribute Hitler's successes to the machinations of a small group of men (and women) who gathered on weekends around Nancy Astor at Cliveden or an equally exclusive all-male intellectual company who collected around the port decanter at All Souls, Oxford, periodically advising the Prime Minister and his Foreign Secretary. Churchill knew a secret he was prepared to share: the blame for Hitler had to be widely distributed among those who led the democracies during the 1930s—the "locust years," in his imaginative chronology—but also among those who had so uncritically accepted their leadership.

Churchill was in a strong position to say these things; he had nothing to hide. The mistakes of the 1930s could not be laid at his door. Ousted from political office in 1929 when the Labour Party formed a government, and kept out even after the Conservative Party, his party, joined the National Government in 1931, Churchill had the dubious distinction of being the most prominent Conservative ex-minister, a former Chancellor of the Exchequer who sat as a backbencher for almost a decade when his party was in office. Churchill's influence was negligible; the little reputation he enjoyed came from his ability to move a few young men by the power of his rhetoric and the force of his argument. His was a lone voice in the House of Commons, warning very early what Hitler was compassing, why Britain ought to bestir itself.

To compare that period, or that life, with what happened in the 1980s in the United States and, more specifically, in the career of someone moving relentlessly to the top, George Bush, is to believe Marx's aphorism that history repeats itself, first as tragedy, then as comedy. If the 1980s are one day seen as "the years the locust hath eaten," there will be no Republican, in or out of office, and no Democrat, in the House or the Senate, who will be able to claim prescience in the Churchillian mold. The individual least entitled to the honor is the man who branded Saddam Hussein the aggressor in Kuwait—which he was—and then proceeded to plot war against him.

The stage had been set much earlier. George Bush, as Vice President, was the willing accomplice and loyal disciple of a President who gulled the nation. The Reagan White House was morally corrupt; those who were close to Reagan knew him to be ideologically simplistic and intellectually barren, particularly in the area of foreign policy. They also knew him to be a consummate politician, a born actor, able to generate sympathy and enthusiasm and to win elections. Bush, a silent Vice President in the tradition of Richard Nixon under Dwight Eisenhower, expected to succeed him as his anointed heir. His assignment was to say little, do nothing, and wait for the happy event that would make his residential address the best in the nation, 1600 Pennsylvania Avenue.

During eight years of the Iraq-Iran war, when Iraq was the aggressor, the Reagan administration secretly and cynically shipped arms to both belligerents. Through various channels, it also shared intelligence information, which the Iranians found substantially less useful than the Iraqis. There is nothing to suggest that the Vice President found any of these policies offensive or recommended others. Present at all the major meetings at which the Iran-Contra conspiracy—the administration's secret exchange of arms for hostages—was taking shape, the Vice President never spoke on the matter, according to all reports. If he recognized the hazard to the President and the greater danger to the nation, he kept silent. Once free of the constraints of the vice presidency, his own "boss" in the

White House, he showed the same lack of insight, the same lethargy, the same caution. He never took in what Iraq's experience in the 1980s had been, why it would not permanently sit on its vast stock of arms. During his own first year and a half as President, the name Saddam Hussein scarcely exited his mouth; Iraq never figured among America's prominent Islamic foes in the way Iran, Libya, and Syria at one time or another did.

While America's enemies in the Middle East changed with almost every calendar year, President Bush's silence on the region's problems was not wholly accidental. It showed his habitual intellectual sloth and failure to anticipate events and to prepare for them. Despite his years of training in the United Nations, the Central Intelligence Agency, and the White House, the President knew little about the region. Politically ambitious, but a novice in foreign affairs, he was indifferent to the moral implications of what he or others around him proposed to do.

Having no interest in providing foreign policy instruction to the nation on Iraq, indeed having a compelling political reason for not doing so, he chose the path of caution. To speak too openly about Iraq, about the Gulf more generally, was to risk reminding citizens of the Near East policies of the Reagan administration, particularly of a clandestine arms-for-hostages agreement which, though hotly denied, would not bear new scrutiny. Appropriating the Churchill mantle, the President, in one stroke, erased all that the Reagan administration and his own had done to create Saddam Hussein.

Margaret Thatcher, Churchill's self-appointed political legatee, blessed the Bush enterprise; so did the United Nations. What additional imprimatur could the American people ask for? Saddam had crossed a border and taken away a nation's independence. Could more be said about his perfidy? George Bush, the President, implied that he was simply doing in 1990 what Churchill, had he been in office, would have done to Nazi Germany as early as 1935. An aggressive dictator, whom the administration took care never to characterize as Arab—the Coalition, after all, included "good" Arabs—was plotting the military domination of the Gulf, hoping to control its oil resources, thereby strangling the industrial world. The international community was summoned to stop him, with George Bush in command.

But Iraq was not Germany, and the President wildly exaggerated its military power from the first day. There is abundant evidence to suggest that he never expected (or intended) sanctions to work, and that from an early date he resisted the efforts of "outsiders" to negotiate an Iraqi withdrawal from Kuwait, hoping that he would be able to exhibit the resolve his public image so lacked, allowing him to address the matter militarily. Perhaps most grievously, he never took either the American public or the Congress into his confidence, never believing it necessary to be straightforward with either.

Did the President's "desire for popularity and electoral success irrespective of the interests of the State"—as Churchill had written so perceptibly of the politicians in the context of the 1930s—blind him to the long-range foreign policy interests of the United States? Could he even understand these interests, given his life experience as a child of World War II, the Cold War, and the White House, as it came to be in the time of Richard Nixon and Ronald Reagan? Was his political use of the Munich analogy, for example, not a calculated effort to conceal his own eighteen-month failure to attend to grave domestic difficulties, and also an even more serious ten-year failure of two Republican administrations to cope imaginatively with major foreign policy dilemmas? Did he, like his predecessor, lack all comprehension of the world of the late twentieth century, having only a very slight purchase on the hazards that lurked, and not only in the Middle East, and the opportunities that beckoned, and not only in Eastern Europe? Was he, in short, like so many other advantaged Americans of his generation, incapable of shedding his nineteenth-century provincialisms, which marked him as an old-fashioned man, still unable to take in the tragic events of his own century, which he neither experienced nor understood?

The President's failure to be more open about his policies, to show greater forthrightness in explaining what he proposed to do, suggested a domestic political motive that went considerably beyond his advertised foreign policy concern to liberate Kuwait, protect the Saudis, and guarantee the free flow of oil from the Gulf. The President's reticences, in the circumstances, were extraordinary. Churchill could never have conceived of using such lame explanations to defend a commitment of forces as large as those announced by the President after the November election, nor could he have been so cavalier in making the Coalition, cobbled together by the President and his hard-traveling Secretary of State, seem so insipid. Questions would have been raised in Parliament; the press would have demanded explanations, embarrassingly recalling all manner of things said and done in the past. Neither happened in the United States. Congress was in recess during the most critical period; the media, with a few admirable exceptions, seemed almost thrilled by the drama coming out of the White House, and perceived the situation in terms of Vietnam, noting the great numbers of American casualties that would almost certainly be suffered in any Gulf war. The President, knowing his own intentions, was not unhappy to see the debate center on these issues. They played into his hands, serving his political ends.

Bush, through his many experiences in or close to the White House, knew something of the American public's tolerance for presidential game playing. Ronald Reagan, in his moral preachings and perpetual storytelling, created fictions that even his staff saw no reason to correct. Theodore Roosevelt's principle of using the White House as a "bully pulpit," carried into the late twentieth century, came to mean an invitation to transmit myths that flattered the public and extolled the President. This mutual back scratching provided an admirable setting for the portrayal of virtue and vice. After August 2, the Kuwaitis were virtuous, the Iraqis vicious, and the President, an impartial judge in the matter, appeared as the sheriff who would enforce the law.

The speech carried from the Oval Office on the morning of August 8—the President saw no need to deliver it in prime time—was the conventional mythic address that Ronald Reagan might just as easily have delivered, with no less effect. *The New York Times*—the "newspaper of record"—did not publish the text; nor did it appear in *The Washington Post*. The work of a hack, someone assigned to do a chore of no importance, it substituted cliché for argument, exhortation for analysis. The speech began: "In the life of a nation, we're called upon to define who we are and what we believe. Sometimes these choices are not easy. But today as President, I ask for your support in a decision I've made to stand up for what's right and condemn what's wrong—all in the cause of peace."

Had the speech been written essentially for an audience of dedicated daytime television watchers, or could the President be serious in insisting that his one purpose in mobilizing the 82nd Airborne Division and key units of the United States Air Force was to defend American principles, and, of course, the Saudi Arabian homeland? Bush used the language of World War II; the Iraqi armed forces "stormed in blitzkrieg fashion through Kuwait in a few short hours." The aggression, he said, "came just hours after Saddam Hussein specifically assured numerous countries in the area that there would be no invasion." Saddam had lied, the President intoned solemnly. It was a theme to which he would revert frequently in the days ahead.

"We succeeded in the struggle for freedom in Europe because we and our allies remained stalwart," the President told the nation. "Keeping the peace in the Middle East will require no less. We're beginning a new era. This new era can be full of promise. An age of freedom. A time of peace for all people. But if history teaches us anything, it is that we must resist aggression or it will destroy our freedoms. Appeasement does not work. As was the case in the 1930s, we see in Saddam Hussein an aggressive dictator threatening his neighbors. Only fourteen days ago Saddam Hussein promised his friends he would not invade Kuwait. And four days ago he promised the world he would withdraw. And twice we have seen what his promises mean. His promises mean nothing."

A final excerpt may suggest the quality of the President's argument. He said: "Standing up for our principles will not come easy. It may take time and possibly cost a great deal. But we are asking no more of anyone than of the brave young men and women of our armed forces and their families. And I ask that in the churches around the country prayers be said for those who are committed to protect and defend America's interests." One imagines that in his numerous telephone conversations with foreign heads of state, the President used much more compelling arguments to explain what the United States was doing and why it needed foreign assistance. But in the explanations given the American public, he represented himself as Churchill, boldly confronting the naked aggression of a dictator whose soldiers "raped" Kuwait and reduced to ruins the great modern city built on oil revenues.

Bush's appropriation of a Churchill disguise was effective. The fact that the President had never recognized the dangers of Iraq—had never warned about them in the way Churchill had consistently done about Nazi Germany's aggressive intentions—was almost irrelevant. Nor did it matter that Churchill, in resisting "appeasement," took an immensely unpopular position, supported by only a tiny segment of the British electorate; the majority were much more partial to the policies of Chamberlain, with his promise of "peace in our time." Bush, with a flawless political strategy, based on the principle of simplicity and concealment—which an unfriendly critic might characterize as one of willful deception—avoided any analysis that might have been instructive to the nation.

Had the President wished to take the American people into
his confidence, had he imagined that there was a need for him
to do so, an advantage to be gained—had his concern been
with world order, with something more urgent than his own
reelection in 1992—had he lived in a political environment
different from the one he had come to know under his two
principal Republican Party benefactors, Richard Nixon and
Ronald Reagan, a different speech might have come out of the
Oval Office. Indeed, in view of the importance of the Iraqi
invasion, it might have been delivered in prime time, announced a day in advance to generate excitement, guaranteeing
a large television audience. The text of such a speech would
have been carried in *The New York Times*; one would have heard
of it in the European Community; it would have resonated in
the Arab world. No such speech was given in the first days of
August, or indeed at any later date, because no one in the
White House, in the presidential entourage, thought it
necessary.

It was impossible for the President to acknowledge what
everyone abroad knew to be true: that had he not interposed
the American forces at the time he did, no other country would
have done so. The European Community, despite its reputed
and real economic strength, was certainly not inclined to mount
such a response, and not simply because it had no defense
policy adequate to coping with a crisis like the one created by
Iraq's invasion of Kuwait. Though the President never mentioned Israel, the world knew that Israel's sole defender was
the United States. While the United States and all the other
great powers could abide hundreds of thousands of casualties
in an eight-year war between Iran and Iraq, the American
President could not gaze with equal equanimity on a surprise
attack by Iraq on Israel, or, to avoid that, a sudden preemptive
attack by Israel on Iraq.

The first, if it happened, could produce tens of thousands
of casualties in Tel Aviv in a single night. Saddam Hussein's

Scud missiles, flying over Jordan from secure bases in Iraq or Kuwait, could do Israel untold damage, creating a crisis of major proportions in the Middle East, and also in the United States. If Israel, to avert such a catastrophe, struck first, the administration would be confronted with a less serious crisis at home but a more grave situation internationally. An Israeli attack on Iraq's atomic, biological, and chemical weapons facilities would have had consequences more fateful than those experienced by Reagan and his colleagues when Israel took out Iraq's nuclear capability in 1981. Whatever sympathy individual European states like Great Britain, France, Germany, or Italy might on occasion express for Israel, a grievous military disaster in that country, while regrettable, would not have generated major political repercussions elsewhere unless it led to prolonged general war in the region. For other countries, Japan and China, for example, not to speak of the Soviet Union and any number of neutral states in Asia and Africa, Israel's welfare, and indeed its survival, counted for little.

The President chose not to speak of any of them. An act of discretion? In part, but also an expression of his unwillingness to take the nation into his confidence, to use the Iraqi invasion to educate the American public about the Middle East and also about arms pollution in the world and nationalisms that paraded under the banner of religious and patriotic revival. To advertise the full extent of the hazards in the Kuwaiti situation would have been to exacerbate the situation, creating even greater panic in New York and in stock exchanges around the world.

There was yet another reason for the President's silence about these matters. He hoped to create a military Coalition that would include a number of Arab states. Any reference to Israel, he imagined, would threaten that Coalition. Bush was well aware that the Saudis were terrified of Iraq, but not so much so that he could afford to say that both Saudi Arabia and Israel were threatened by Iraq. The Coalition was thought to be so fragile, and the hostility to Israel so intense in the Muslim world, that any such impolitic statement would cause the Coalition to fall apart instantly. Indeed, the President's reticences extended to other subjects as well. He had no interest, for example, in enlightening the American public about past events in the Middle East. He could speak of the Iraqi invasion of Kuwait as both unjustified and unprovoked, but could not go on to say that a decade earlier, in 1980, Iraq had received massive financial support from both Kuwait and Saudi Arabia in its war against Iran. Both became, in effect, the principal "bankers" of Saddam in his unprovoked aggression against the Ayatollah Khomeini. To intrude with such details, even to suggest them, was to complicate the story unnecessarily.

"Irangate" was only one of several subjects the President had no wish to remind the nation of. To rehearse again—or give a new and more accurate version of the tale of America's relations with Iran since the expulsion of the Shah—would be to open a larger can of worms. The Ayatollah Khomeini's problems with the United States were purportedly all of his own making; the bigoted anti-American Islamic fundamentalist who had kept American Embassy hostages imprisoned for over a year, and had excoriated American imperialism and decadence on every occasion, merited no sympathy. When Iraq, a Soviet ally and client state, invaded Iran, the United States looked away. Officially, the United States was neutral. In fact, in various ways and at different times, it helped one or the other, doing so covertly in all instances, pretending not to care a whit whether the war continued or ended. The United States never seriously sought to make peace between the two; having no official diplomatic relations with either, it operated through others, useful intermediaries who could be relied on to transmit American arms or intelligence.

As the Iran-Iraq war proceeded, becoming increasingly brutal and inhumane, reports of large-scale military slaughter reached the outside world. When chemical weapons came to be used by Iraq, and exchanges of missiles damaged cities on both sides of the border, the world watched; only occasionally, and principally through the United Nations, were efforts made to bring the war to an end. The Arab League tried at times, with scant success. Americans, like so many others, looked on from the outside, watching the two tear at each other, using weapons of mass destruction supplied overwhelmingly from abroad.

Nor would the President's political objectives, so admirably served by Iraq's invasion of Kuwait, gain from the American public's learning that no equivalent American (or world) outrage had attended Iraq's invasion of Iran a decade earlier. Then there had been no condemnation of Iraq for its violation of international law, its disregard of the United Nations Charter. The violent and savage rhetoric the Ayatollah used, not only against the United States but also against rich Islamic countries like Saudi Arabia and Kuwait for their religious and moral transgressions, made them willing accomplices of Iraq in its war against Iran. In effect, the Saudis and Kuwaitis hired Saddam Hussein to do their military work, to stave off the political disaster they feared from possible insurrection at home. Both pretended that Iraq, in invading Iran, was simply making a contribution to peace in the Gulf. Each, fearing the Ayatollah, made considerable sums of money and substantial amounts of war matériel available to the Iraqis, believing that Iran's defeat was in the interest of all Arab peoples. This was not a tale that President Bush had any interest in telling.

Without these large gifts of money and military equipment, Iraq would not have been able to sustain its war; even with such assistance, and with continued aid from the Soviet Union, Iraq's longtime ally, Iraq failed to capitalize on its initial military successes. Its original invasion was repulsed and much of the captured Iranian territory lost; the war stalemated. Year after year, new offensives were undertaken on the ground, with no conclusive results; casualties, in dead and wounded, reached obscene levels. Still, the war went on. Iran, able to drive the Iraqi armies back, could not proceed to win the decisive victory it sought. The Iraqi leadership, increasingly frustrated by its military reverses, devastated its own people, including the large Kurdish minority within its frontiers. No less fierce with its enemies, the Iraqis used poison gas repeatedly, imagining that this would cause Iran to capitulate. Again, they were wrong.

For the President to have told this story would have been to instruct the American people in a matter they rarely reflected on: Islamic rivalry was endemic; in a single decade, Iraq had managed to wage aggressive war against two Islamic states, conquering one, being stalemated in its effort to defeat the other. Now the Saudis were threatened. So also were the Israelis; Saddam had pledged the destruction of Israel. A dictator capable of such repeated military aggression was a threat to the world. But to speak of more than Kuwait and Saudi Arabia would have been to make the President's tale more complex; it might have destroyed the simple symmetry of his Nazi paradigm.

By being so circumspect, however, the President failed to portray with any accuracy the plight of the Iraqi people. Again, he saw no need to do so. What would it profit the American public to know that Iraqis lived in mortal fear of the tyrant who ruled over them, that they were wholly incapable of resisting the power of his army and secret police? Like the Romanian people under Ceauşescu, they lived in terror, for the most part silently. The President preferred to emphasize the one crucial condition in all the United Nations resolutions: Iraq had to leave the territory of Kuwait. All else was secondary.

In the President's concern to make it all seem natural, he neglected to dwell on the quite exceptional circumstances that led the Soviet Union to accept the American initiative against Iraq in the United Nations Security Council. A similar Soviet vote a decade earlier against one of its allies would have been unthinkable. Another individual speaking from the Oval Office might have wished to emphasize the importance of the United Nations and the role it might play in peacekeeping. In the circumstances, the suggestion that the vote in the Security Council only confirmed the wisdom of those who had founded the United Nations in 1945 in San Francisco might have seemed appropriate. For President Bush to have said this, however, would have been to offend a number of prominent Republicans who had never learned to forgive "that man in the White House," Franklin Roosevelt.

Nor, for that matter, did the President see a need to explain his position with respect to sanctions. His political plan suggested that he would do well to support them, and not reveal prematurely his limited patience with such slow-working measures. In this, as in everything else, the President kept his own counsel; it was inconceivable that he would wish to show his hand before the midterm elections, and prepare the country for the day when sanctions would be abandoned in favor of military action. Whatever his views, they were never made public. It was impossible, impolitic, for him to state them, just as a return to the conditions of August 1 was unthinkable. Neither Saudi Arabia nor Israel, watching the Iraqi devastation in Kuwait, could have accepted to live again in some sort of reciprocal tolerance with a dangerously armed Iraq. Yet the United Nations had not made the total disarming of Iraq a condition of the lifting of its sanctions. Arms sales and arms pollution did not figure explicitly in the agenda of issues that had to be settled before Iraq was pardoned. While there had been mention of reparations that Iraq would be obliged to pay Kuwait, the references to arms limitations were considerably more imprecise.

Did President Bush know this? Of course. Did he have any interest in saying it? No. Thinking in other time frames, having quite other objectives, relying wholly on his experience and the advice he received, which reflected overwhelmingly the specific values of the American world he knew—of his own adolescence and early adulthood in World War II and of his mature years in a Cold War world—he reflected very little on twentieth-century war as a tragedy or on peace as an inconceivably difficult thing to fashion, if it involved something more than clearing a territorial space of its aggressor.

Reflection was not George Bush's strong suit, nor was it that of his Secretary of State. Neither had the historical learning or historical imagination that made it possible for Europeans like Churchill or de Gaulle to incorporate incidents of their own lives in a larger conceptual scheme. The President, unlike his immediate predecessor, read the documents and reports submitted to him, but the information they contained did not lead him to think deeply about the country or the world.

Understandably, the President could not bring himself to suggest that the Reagan administration had not lived up to its responsibilities, that, however unwittingly, it had helped create conditions that allowed men like Saddam Hussein to prosper, to rule by terror at home and become a military menace to their neighbors. He dared not acknowledge that in his own eighteen months as President he had been wholly inattentive to the problem of Iraq, that his failure to take Saddam seriously might have contributed in some measure to the crisis that erupted in the first days of August. Presidents are rarely self-critical; they cannot be expected to find fault with their predecessors, particularly when they have been their patrons and sponsors.

In Bush's case, it was particularly difficult for him to acknowledge that there had been failures in either American diplomacy or intelligence. To have questioned the first would have been to criticize, if only by implication, the Secretary of State, James Baker, the President's most intimate friend and colleague, to whom he owed more than he could ever hope to repay. Baker, through inadvertence, had failed the President, being too busy with what he conceived to be more important foreign policy chores. The Middle East never figured high on his agenda, and when he did stop to consider it, putting aside his obviously more interesting and important Soviet brief, his attention was generally focused on Israel, the PLO, and what was euphemistically called the peace process. Neither in his efforts to warn and advise, nor in his perceptions of the nature of the crisis brewing in the Middle East, had Baker given adequate instruction to the President on Middle Eastern flash points. In Mrs. Thatcher's Britain, Lord Carrington, the Foreign Secretary, having failed in a comparable crisis to alert the Prime Minister to the Argentinian danger to the Falklands, paid for his mistake by resigning from the Cabinet. No one, least of all the President, called for the same sacrifice of office on Baker's part. Having committed no error—at least in the President's mind—why should he be chastised or penalized?

Wrapping himself securely in the American flag—a tactic that he learned to use to his advantage early in his political career and that he exploited with remarkable skill in his electoral campaign against Michael Dukakis—the President recognized that he required only a single, very simple theme constantly reiterated. He called on the nation to support its brave boys and girls, men and women, all prepared to make the supreme sacrifice in the cause of justice and peace.

The President and his Secretary of State, who quickly returned from Siberia to join him in helping with the Coalition building and alms begging that became an integral part of their joint operation, were a remarkable team, ably abetted after the war began by the Secretary of Defense and the Chairman of the Joint Chiefs of Staff. In splitting the Arab world, creating a fissure where none had existed previously, they created a myth that bore little relation to reality. Syria had been unable to abide Iraq for decades; Hafez al-Assad was Saddam's sworn enemy. Egypt, ostracized by other Arab states for a decade after the Camp David accords, had tried persistently to renew relations with the oil-rich Saudis. Alliances and cleavages in the Arab world were common. These, however, were minor details, of the kind Ronald Reagan habitually ignored; George Bush was capable of the same kind of selective memory. Indeed, he was sufficiently circumspect in what he chose to say about the Middle East so that he never acknowledged that one of his purposes was to construct a new pro-American Arab coalition, based on Saudi Arabia, Egypt, and Syria, which, it was to be hoped, would give him the support necessary to force Israel to submit to what Americans perceived to be satisfactory peace terms.

The fact that an old Arab friend of the United States, King Hussein of Jordan, was shelved, punished for not joining in condemning Saddam, seemed just and reasonable to those who could imagine no valid excuse for any Arab (or other) state refusing to cooperate with the Coalition. The Jordanian king and his military advisers, preoccupied with their own vocal and powerful Palestinian population demonstrating for a Saddam victory in the streets of Amman, were dismissed as craven, or worse. All loyal friends of the United States were expected to demonstrate their support in the same fashion. Americans, in actively resisting Iraqi aggression, in taking on the burdens of others, insisted that the only valid issue was Iraq's illegal invasion. Frontiers were sacred; regimes were inconsequential; the lives of enemy soldiers, civilians, and subject peoples figured little in the calculus of a great power committed to peace through war. It was a masterful political performance, a public relations stunt worthy of the Great Communicator himself, who would certainly have believed every word of the well-worn argument. If victory came through Saddam's withdrawal, Bush risked nothing; if it came after a short, successful war, it would secure his reelection.

# President Reagan:
# The Sorcerer

R onald Reagan's White House was George Bush's political nursery. The Vice President, in his fifties, touted for his long service abroad and at home, actually knew little about the world and even less about his own country. The President, unwittingly, unintentionally, provided instruction in both, though not of the traditional kind. Service under Ronald Reagan taught the younger man that the game of American politics was played by essentially two rules: electoral victory was the only thing that mattered and moral uplift was a potent opiate, more powerful than prosaic truth. The Vice President, observing the President, realized that foreign policy was a luxury; the United States, even in the last part of the twentieth century, could do without it, though it could not do without the pretense of it. The political genius of the President lay in his remarkable capacity to pretend to be reshaping the world, initially in the Middle East, later with the Soviet Union. Both were fables, largely self-invented, at least in the form given by the President.

Neither President Reagan nor his advisers produced any major breakthroughs in the Middle East, none comparable to the modest but real successes achieved under Presidents Nixon and Carter. Though much was made of the President's second-term diplomatic accomplishments with Mikhail Gorbachev, these were exaggerated; Soviet accommodation to the purposes of others derived largely from changes forced on the Kremlin by a Soviet economy that was in crisis and by a satellite empire that had lost the fear of its ruler's power. The President, instructed by his great and good friend Margaret Thatcher, who arrived with the glad tidings that there was now a man in the Kremlin with whom one could hope to do business, in effect embraced the idea of détente, though he of course never called it that. Summitry was the answer, and the Vice President learned that frequent encounters between the world's two great leaders produced substantial political bonuses.

The President taught him another lesson: the power of myth, the capacity of an accomplished storyteller to give the illusion of having caused great events to happen. The President knew how to develop a story line, and the public, prepared to believe it, scarcely recognized the hand of the accomplished political artist. An even greater skill was passed on to the Vice President: to avoid public scandal, covering one's tracks when one was caught in a delicate and potentially dangerous situation, involved more than the capacity to prevaricate or tell a tall tale. It required the skills of the theater—a memorizing of lines, obviously, but also a sense of the audience, of how it could be managed and manipulated. Richard Nixon never learned how to do this; uncomfortable in the presence of strangers, fearful of individuals he knew were seeking to entrap him, he showed his unease, thereby encouraging suspicion. President Reagan, having no fears of those seated before him, least of all the press, estimated their abilities correctly and showed his theatrical talent, most conspicuously in the Irangate affair. Here Bush learned that a President could conceal the truth when it was known to only a very few who would themselves be incriminated were it to be revealed.

Although George Bush arrived in the White House as Vice President with little knowledge of foreign policy, this did not preclude his being taken to be an expert in the field. Credentials as a former United States Ambassador to the United Nations and a former Director of the Central Intelligence Agency, not to speak of service in Mao's China, in Beijing, were thought to have provided ample international experience. A critical examination of his record in all these appointive offices, under Presidents Nixon and Ford, would have revealed a curious fact. None of the positions provided great scope for action; they required him to look the part, sit and be patient, enjoy the perquisites of office, and show himself obedient and loyal.

As Ambassador to the United Nations in President Nixon's administration, when Henry Kissinger served as foreign policy strategist-in-chief, the Vice President found little occasion to test his intellectual or diplomatic powers, let alone hone them. Neither Nixon nor Kissinger intended for their man in New York to take the initiative on matters of consequence. Neither prized his understanding of foreign policy issues or imagined that his luxurious Waldorf-Astoria aerie allowed him access to the basic information they required for reaching policy decisions. The ambassador was someone to give orders to, not someone to seek advice from. When a crisis arose, as in the India-Pakistan war, all direction came from the White House.

After brief service as chairman of the Republican National Committee, coinciding with the difficult days in Washington when it appeared that President Nixon might be impeached, Bush was given another diplomatic assignment, this time by President Ford to the People's Republic of China, to serve as chief of the United States Liaison Office. Again, through no fault of his, the post gave George Bush negligible experience. If Bush's later boss, Ronald Reagan, complained of too many Kremlin leaders dying on him, Bush had cause to bemoan the opposite; Mao, the hero of the Chinese revolution, refused to die. Everything was "on hold" so long as the old leader lived;

there was little the American chief of mission could do. China was not unpleasant duty—nothing Bush ever did seemed unpleasant or burdensome—but it provided little occasion for diplomatic jousting, let alone intellectual development. Still, he returned from his brief service a "China expert."

In his next political incarnation, as Director of the Central Intelligence Agency—a post he held for scarcely more than a year—George Bush was appointed with a specific task: to do nothing. President Ford, alarmed that the coveted Republican Party presidential nomination might be taken away from him by resurgent conservative forces in the country partial to the candidacy of Ronald Reagan, gave the CIA post to Bush with the explicit understanding that he would avoid attracting media or congressional attention to the beleaguered Agency. The President knew his man; he chose wisely. Recognizing how harmful earlier disclosures about the CIA had been, and not only in Congress, the President hoped that there would be no new disclosures, no additional Agency scandals to divert the public or jeopardize his own political standing. The task—to "keep the lid" on the Agency, restoring morale, if possible, but doing nothing to attract attention to himself or his province— suited him perfectly.

For complex personal and intellectual reasons, Bush had little interest in and no capacity for conceiving or executing large and ambitious projects. Neither was expected of him in his CIA post; he enjoyed the title of Director and the perquisites of office. Indeed, he would have gladly stayed on under Jimmy Carter—believing it essential that the post no longer be thought political—but Carter had no need of his services. The history of the nation would have been different had Bush been retained by the new President. He might have served a real term, admired for affability and accessibility, a gentleman of the old school, redolent of Allen Dulles.

In 1977, Bush, like other Republican appointees, found himself unemployed. Without a profession, having no legal practice or business to return to, he decided to sit out the Democratic years in his "native" Texas, in the company of his friend James Baker 3rd, who had just managed President Ford's unsuccessful electoral campaign. Bush could look back on four presidential assignments, all honorably completed, which gave him some prominence in the Republican Party, the same superficial name recognition with the public that came to others enjoying such positions in a television age. Bush had added titles to his name, a skill he first acquired in his years at Phillips Andover Academy. With a limited political background, lacking, except for two terms in Congress, experience as an elected official, with a curriculum vitae of impressive citations that concealed more than they told, George Bush entered the White House as the man selected by Ronald Reagan to serve as Vice President.

There, for eight years, though he learned little about foreign policy, he was instructed in how to manipulate the media. Privileged to participate in meetings of the National Security Council, he sat and listened; briefed by his own staff and others, particularly when the President was in the hospital or otherwise absent from the capital, he picked up some of the techniques of White House government; fed gossip and rumor by James Baker, the Chief of Staff in the President's first term, he knew the most intimate details about the strange and bizarre kingdom Ronald Reagan presided over. As the President's constant choice to go on foreign missions, mostly to represent him on great state occasions—principally funerals and memorial services that the President chose to avoid, perhaps out of a desire not to be reminded of his own mortality—Bush became superficially acquainted with many of the political leaders then prominent on the world scene.

All this frenetic public activity, occasionally shown on the television screen when the cameras could be taken away even for a few minutes from the principal actor, the President, substituted not at all for the kind of foreign policy instruction

Richard Nixon received as Dwight Eisenhower's Vice President. The difference, in a word, was the President himself. Ronald Reagan knew nothing about foreign policy, and had nothing to teach George Bush, if instruction is conceived as involving the ability to conceptualize problems, weigh evidence, and make decisions. Reagan's own habit was to tell stories, make public appearances, and take direction from his staff. Dialogue was not his habit; discussion was not his pleasure; intellectual wrestling was not his indoor sport. If the Vice President wished for instruction in foreign policy, he would have to look elsewhere.

In theory, there were any number of foreign policy nannies about, particularly in the White House, to instruct the Vice President in the more abstruse aspects of the issues. In this, however, Bush was unlucky. Under Ronald Reagan, the post of National Security Adviser became a rotating one, the most accident-prone in the federal government. There were almost as many National Security advisers during Reagan's two terms of office as there were calendar years, more indeed than there had been in all the time since Harry Truman occupied the Oval Office. Whether the impermanence reflected the President's ignorance of the subject or his bad judgment in choosing individuals, foreign policy was an area where a new man was constantly being broken in. In this, as in so many other things, Ronald Reagan set a record.

Inevitably, George Bush, as Vice President, learned from observing the President, at National Security Council and other meetings, where he himself sat silently. Rumor, spread by the Vice President's loyal staff, suggested that he spoke his mind at his private Thursday lunches with the President. Since no one knew what he said, one could only wonder what intelligence he provided the President, what confidences he shared, why he should be so open with the President alone when he was so silent when others were present. In fact, there is good reason to believe that he fawned on the President, as all others in the White House did, and said little to disturb or distress him.

Yet the Vice President knew a great deal about the political and social intrigues that James Baker kept him informed about. Baker, in his White House position in the first Reagan term, enjoyed unusual access to the President, strengthened, it was said, by the First Lady's approval of his manner and manners. Baker, in her view, was a gentleman. Whether Baker and Bush together, in the privacy of their offices, did more than gossip and plot, it is impossible to know. Prepared to serve till the happy day when they were themselves served, each, in his own way, was positioning himself for the presidency.

Glancing at the man who held it, they knew they could do as well, particularly if they took instruction in the only art he completely mastered, American politics. The President knew things they did not know; to be his pupil made sense. The Vice President learned from watching the President; the same experience, in the mind of a Saint-Simon, would have provided an incomparable court history. For George Bush, it only confirmed what many outside knew; the President, an aged man when he assumed his title, occasionally an invalid, always indolent and frequently inattentive, occupied an office in which frenetic activity was taken for granted and contemplation was uncommon, in which leisure was regulated by strict daily appointment schedules. The President violated all the rules; like many old rich men, and some not so old, he enjoyed his comforts. His ample staff existed to cater to his needs, and his wife made certain they did. Bush was more than ready to cooperate.

The Vice President, observing the President, learned a valuable lesson: politics, in the last part of the twentieth century, relied on deception, the kind that a television camera never captured, that made a man appear innocent even when he was guilty, but, more importantly, represented him in ways that bore little relation to the truth. Ronald Reagan on camera was not the man known to his staff, his professional valets. An old boy of the Midwest—a fact of some consequence to the staid Connecticut Yankee observing him—born in exceedingly modest circumstances, the President had overcome the disadvantage of a childhood spent in the company of an unstable father who drank too much. Achieving early fame as an actor, profiting from the value Americans attached to good looks, he starred in B films and later in television, where he celebrated American virtue.

Amassing a modest fortune, sufficient to buy a ranch and do all those other things appropriate to someone of wealth and position, as California defined both, Ronald Reagan understood and empathized with "middle America," his own America. Even marriage to a snob did nothing to deflect him from his faith in a democracy pledged to a social equality he himself did nothing to foster. Knowing little of the world outside the United States, and having no desire to learn its reputed mysteries, he began his political apprenticeship at a very high level, as governor of California. From there, with the help of many good and very rich friends, he made his way to the White House. It was a remarkable political odyssey, a twentieth-century version of the nineteenth-century American log cabin caricature, but the President, through artful selection, could make it seem Everyman's tale. George Bush would try to do the same with his own far more sheltered American upbringing.

The man called the Great Communicator by the media knew how to exploit every photo opportunity, as Donald Regan, his later White House Chief of Staff, revealed in embarrassing detail. More important, however, was the care the President and his wife gave to seeing themselves and their purported values presented in a way calculated to win public approval. Bush watched all this, and may have divined a small but precious secret: the American people enjoyed a President who flattered them, knew how to make himself appealing, fabricated tall tales, and cared not at all to instruct, to bore with unnecessary and distressing details of a kind he himself preferred not to know. Using humor, affability, voice, and a nonchalant manner to achieve his political ends, the President created a sense of well-being among those who knew him, if only from the intimacy of the television screen.

Bush, lacking these same qualities of personality, could not suddenly develop them, but he could ask himself how he might shape his image to appeal to the people as the President did, though sharing little of his charm and none of his pretended (or real) innocence. For this President belonged to the people and appeared to share their dreams in a way that other of his Republican predecessors, and not only the ill-starred Richard Nixon, never could. Practicing the fine art of concealment, but also others that depended on a polished act as a principled man of probity, he excelled as a fabulator. The Vice President also learned from him how to use rhetoric—the rhetoric of religion, ambiguously Christian—to emphasize and celebrate American virtue. To speak of "crusades" was as important as to speak of "wars," and to do both in the name of a holy American mission was to do more than make a ritual presidential deference to God and the divine.

The President, mean and stingy himself, as even the new rich may occasionally be, knew those traits to be widely and generally distributed in the population. Bush, from his own genteel Yankee experience, knew the same truth. He understood why no one had to hand the President cue cards to suggest how palatable massive tax cuts would be. A deep suspicion of the federal government's interfering ways had helped elect Carter to the White House. It served a second time with Reagan. Why should it not do the same for Bush one day, when he, like others in the Republican Party, habitually equated federal expenditure with governmental waste?

And if the federal budgets were not immediately pared, in part because of large appropriations to build absolutely necessary defenses against the Soviet threat, the President ignored these expenses, dwelling instead on the excessive spending authorized by the House of Representatives, controlled by the Democrats. The President had not yet been able wholly to

bridle unruly liberals, to cure them of their insatiable appetite
for waste, their miserable spendthrift habits. As the federal
deficit grew, those who believed as the President did, and their
number was legion, expected economic growth and new incentives to investment to provide taxable income to reduce deficits
and create a new level of American prosperity. When his
policies failed to achieve the first, though many in the middle
class grew rich and sleek, the President simply ignored the
evidence. Silence was a virtue when speech betrayed a lack of
faith.

Whether the Vice President believed in these theories—he
claimed to be something of an economist, having studied the
subject as an undergraduate at Yale—he was never indiscreet
enough to voice reservations, let alone express dissent. He had
no reason to wish to go his own way, as David Stockman and
others did, using their few years in the service of the President
to build vast fortunes in the smaller world outside. George
Bush had no need of money; he had arrived in the one place
he longed to be in, and there was no reason for him to leave;
he simply wished to move upstairs.

The country became increasingly prosperous, with many
millions earning unprecedented real dollar incomes. Though
unemployment soared to 9.7 percent in 1982, the highest since
1941, the President, calm and unperturbed, believed that the
situation would correct itself. It did, long before the 1984
elections, the crucial date on his political calendar. While
millions shared not at all in the new prosperity, they were
largely invisible, or thought to be. In any case, they did not
habitually vote. The President, like his friend the British Prime
Minister, committed to a rhetoric of self-help, argued for a
retreat from the left-wing permissiveness of another era. The
Vice President joined in celebrating their achievement, rewarded in the currency he esteemed: political success. The
pocketbook, he knew, weighed more heavily than ephemeral
and elusive foreign policy victories.

By November 1984, the "recession" was a distant memory. The President's second-term victory over Walter Mondale, a landslide, gave him a popular vote as decisive as any that Roosevelt registered in his four bids for the presidency; it compared favorably with that of other recent Presidents; neither Eisenhower nor Kennedy, Truman nor Carter enjoyed comparable electoral success. Indeed, the only two who did were Lyndon Johnson, defeating Barry Goldwater in 1964, and Richard Nixon, smashing George McGovern in 1972.

The Vice President recognized that foreign affairs initiatives did not translate into votes. Why, then, be concerned with them? The President, to the limited extent that he *was* concerned, seemed only to be seeking escape from the boredom and inconclusiveness of domestic politics, with its perpetual obligation to bargain with pressure groups and to deal with obscure men and women in Congress who had to be persuaded to vote a certain way. Foreign affairs became a more interesting and casual enterprise, particularly engrossing and even diverting in a second term when reelection was no longer a presidential concern.

The President, who started his first term speaking ill of the Soviet Union, the "evil empire," managed a remarkable about-face, almost a Damascus-like conversion, in his last four years. In his second summit with Gorbachev, at Reykjavik, Iceland, the President deluded himself into believing that the two had come close to creating the nuclear-free world that all mankind pined for. It was truly exhilarating, and only Gorbachev's insistence that the United States abandon its Strategic Defense Initiative—in the President's mind a purely defensive system —caused the Reykjavik summit to fail. It is doubtful that the Vice President, knowing the President, imagined that anything like this "breakthrough" either had happened or had been impending. In any case, he remained silent, noting what "summitry" could do to establish a President's reputation as a man of peace, committed to freedom.

The fact that America's principal NATO allies saw the Reykjavik summit as a disaster narrowly averted, that James Schlesinger, former Secretary of Defense and Director of the CIA, shared those views and expressed them more guardedly in *Foreign Affairs*, suggested that the summit—ill prepared and ill conceived—left the President vulnerable. The Vice President would have placed his political career in jeopardy had he advanced the same argument in the privacy of a Thursday lunch. The President lived in the illusion that he had performed exceptionally well at Reykjavik; he had come within an inch of achieving a major diplomatic triumph. His sycophant-servants were expected to agree. Only those without political interests —certainly none comparable to that of a man who aspired to succeed him—could afford to tell him the truth. Abroad, Michael Howard, Regius Professor of History at Oxford, said it all when he wrote: "Reykjavik succeeded in alienating virtually every sector of European public opinion."

Allied public opinion was not something the Vice President habitually worried about. What interested him was that Reykjavik did not play particularly well in the United States. The rhetorical flourish that led the President to define his prime objective as the elimination of "all ballistic missiles from the face of the earth" by 1996, creating a "world without nuclear weapons," was thought disingenuous. What marred the summit, making it a near-catastrophe, James Schlesinger wrote, was its "casual utopianism and indifferent preparation." Behind these understated remarks lay a profound truth the Vice President understood; the President's "casual utopianism" was not feigned; it was genuine. Whether or not he shared it, coming from a different social background but having lived a comparably narrow and provincial American existence, he saw its political value and necessity. He, too, pretended that all went well in the United States, that all virtue resided in America, and not only for the happy few.

The Vice President knew a great deal about the President.

He knew almost as much about the First Lady, and had his doubts about both, artfully concealing them. His own political future depended on total dissimulation: the President, quite simply, had helped restore the morale of the nation. That was his distinctive service, and it honored him. The Vice President said this, believing it to be true, knowing it to be useful, to himself and the Republican Party.

Bush, like all others inside and outside the White House, knew that the President came with no prior experience of foreign affairs and had no grasp of the subject. Having observed President Nixon, even if from a distance, the Vice President knew that it made a difference whether the Chief Executive understood the nature of foreign policy and sought to shape some sort of policy agenda. Still, if required to choose between the two men, to give his accolade to one or the other, Bush would not have hesitated for a moment. Only one fact mattered: Nixon had failed and Reagan was succeeding. The Vice President understood success; it had been his objective in life from his early school days. Watching Reagan preside at NSC meetings, Bush must occasionally have wondered what he himself would do when he sat at the center of the table as President, as he expected to. Knowing something of the President's indolence and ignorance, he assumed that his own greater youth and energy would give him certain advantages. Not given to introspection, he never asked what principles would guide him, what skills he would call on. He knew the President's deficiencies; the idea that he shared many of them, that his own education was inadequate, that the White House experience had corrupted him, making him the President's disciple, averse to intellectual labor, committed to rhetoric and playacting, never occurred to him.

The media, in their rare criticisms of Reagan, remarked on his more obvious flaws, his four-and-a-half-day workweeks and his capacity to confound fact and fiction. Bush knew something of greater importance: the President, incapable of acting as an interlocutor—a term he would not have used—rarely engaged subordinates in the White House or the Cabinet in sustained or serious policy discussion. In foreign affairs, where White House influence could be decisive, the President was briefed but not consulted, except in the most superficial sense. He signed documents, gave instructions, but rarely engaged in anything that could be mistaken for dialogue, let alone debate. His genius lay in a capacity to look presidential, masking his intellectual incompetence with sage silences, broken only by his remarkable storytelling ability. That he consulted with few seemed not to matter. Indeed, it gave him his protection.

If, in his second term, the investigators of the Irangate scandal, like the journalistic sleuths who searched relentlessly for the "smoking gun" in the Watergate affair, imagined that they were about to puncture a second President's reputation for probity, they were wrong. The President knew and approved of the secret plans to sell arms to Iran in exchange for American hostages. The Vice President, knowing the President, recognized that the media underestimated his native caution. While George Bush certainly knew what Ronald Reagan had been told about the Iran-Contra deal, he also knew that neither the Tower Commission nor the media were at all likely to discover the truth. It was known by too few—themselves also compromised—and that gave the President his security. For the President had achieved what Richard Nixon had pined for, a silent and servile White House. Only he and his political servants knew it all, and their number was minuscule. Being himself privy to the secret, the Vice President understood this.

As the President's able and attentive student, he grasped another, more important truth: there was no reason for the President to fear the media if he knew how to conduct himself in their presence. President Nixon had always wildly overestimated the media's influence; President Reagan learned how easy it was to manage them. Bush, watching, saw that the media greatly exaggerated their power; the wise politician indulged them, joining them in their perpetual self-praise. The President was always more ferocious with vulnerable Democrats than with *The Washington Post*. The Vice President could not fail to be struck by how often the President took the media in. With Watergate always in mind, they dwelled wholly on whether the President did or did not know—which they would never be able to discover because those who knew would never tell— and they missed the real story.

The President had become an untouchable totem. Under Reagan, the presidency became, in effect, a monarchy, but not the imperial one described by the historian Arthur Schlesinger in the time of Richard Nixon, with its excessive claims to presidential prerogative and authority. Reagan's was a monarchy of the people, incarnate in him, the twice-selected and popularly chosen leader, who delegated his authority, though never officially, to a few loyal servants in whom he had absolute confidence. He created them; they served at his pleasure; his pleasure was to be served by them, to have them act as his memory, but also, and more importantly, as his palace guard. He had no wish for them to be his conscience; none of them possessed the moral compass to serve in that capacity, and Ronald Reagan assumed he had no need of such service. Irangate was less the story of a simple colonel and a not so simple admiral as the tale of an arrogant President who wished the operation to succeed, whose own grasp of foreign policy was negligible, and who had no Secretary of State with sufficient clout to deter him, and no other voice to say him nay.

The corruption of the Reagan administration came not so much from illicit covert operations or the secret laundering of funds as from something more insidious, organic to the regime, which the President had no wish to change, which those who profited, including the Vice President, saw no need to change. Those who worked closely with the President knew how little he understood or cared about what was happening around him. While never patronizing him—which would have been politically and personally dangerous—a very small group inside the White House and in certain of the departments micromanaged him. In doing so, they protected him, demeaning themselves in the process, but never in their own eyes, given the service they imagined themselves to be performing for the nation. They participated in a secret play, concealing what they knew, using the President as their chief prop.

The President and his wife were a team; they knew instinctively how to comport themselves in the high office to which destiny had called them. Superficially, it was all theater. Behind the display—the aging monarch and his consort bidding farewell to the press corps as they rode off in the sunset for yet another long weekend at Camp David—lay facts that any White House reporter knew but chose not to emphasize. The President was less than a month away from his seventieth birthday when he took office in January 1981. Franklin Roosevelt was barely over sixty when he died in 1945, after more than twelve years in the White House. John F. Kennedy, like Theodore Roosevelt, had only recently turned forty when he assumed the presidency. Without making too much of the physical and psychological differences between men in their forties and fifties and those of seventy, greater attention ought to have been given Reagan's age. The Vice President never failed to think of it; a heartbeat away from residence in the big house, he never ignored the President's infirmities.

Even if cosseting and cosmetics served to conceal the President's years, with regular exercise and prolonged periods of rest helping to keep his "insides" those of a reputedly much younger man, at least on the testimony of his surgeon, a would-be assassin's bullet, in the first months of his presidential term, ought to have created a certain skepticism about his physical condition. Instead, stories abounded on his rapid and almost miraculous recovery, the sangfroid and good humor he consistently showed, particularly in the presence of his devoted wife. There were endless "human interest" stories, dwelling on his jokes with doctors, nurses, and others required (or allowed) to visit him. The White House message was a simple one: the President was in full command, almost from the first moment. When, occasionally, the media spotlight shifted from the sick room, it focused principally on such "events" as the remarkable gaffe made by the new Secretary of State, General Alexander Haig, at the moment of greatest uncertainty, about his now "being in charge." The truth was that the President's condition was more grave than what was publicly acknowledged; the Vice President knew it; so, also, did all his White House intimates. They, and he, wondered together and separately whether the day of his elevation was not at hand.

No one outside the White House inquired closely into what the President's first months in office, before the assassination attempt, revealed about his habits and preferences. Secretary Haig, one of the first to be dismissed by the President, wrote years later of the first hours of the Reagan administration. A White House claque, with a subtle but clearly defined hierarchy, composed principally of the President's friends from California, with a smattering of other influential figures in the Republican Party, including the Vice President, formed almost immediately. In place on the day of the inaugural, it was a motley crew even to the man who remembered other White House gangs. Haig gave particular attention to two of the President's California cronies, Meese and Deaver; he said less about the Vice President and the President's Chief of Staff.

A more alert observer, less concerned with himself, less dominated by memories of how Nixon had relegated Vice President Agnew to the wings, might have reflected more on George Bush and his intimate friend, James Baker, elevated to a position so close to the President. While the new Vice President, like his predecessors, had no formal constitutional powers outside the ritual of presiding over the Senate, political intelligence passed to him, and daily access to White House information and gossip could be invaluable to him. Haig, concerned only with his own authority and problems, failed to recognize the importance of the new Vice President's position. He would know everything, not because the President confided in him, which he did not, but because the Chief of Staff wished him to know, given his plans for both their futures. George Bush, as Vice President, would not be Spiro Agnew, and Alexander Haig never considered the question of whether influence in the White House, after the first months, lay not more in the Baker-Bush combination than in the Meese-Deaver alliance. Haig looked only at the vulgar pretensions of the two Californians, full of themselves and their position, strutting about, preening themselves; he paid insufficient attention to the two gentlemen from Texas.

The question not asked: what would such arrangements mean for foreign policy? Who would conduct it? What would the President insist on? What might others be allowed to do? Had George Bush or James Baker arrived in the White House with specific foreign policy objectives, they might have sought to intrude surreptitiously and involve themselves. Because neither knew very much about the subject and cared even less, their gaze fell wholly on the matter crucial to themselves: their own political advancement. While Secretary of State Haig dreamed of novel foreign policy initiatives, of becoming a greater Henry Kissinger, their ambitions were to ingratiate themselves with the President, preparing for their own futures. What both Bush and Baker learned very early was that Haig was not one of their own; bumptious and aggressive, he appeared to have designs on the White House himself. Given their own interests, that was a fatal ambition. Such a man, by definition, was untrustworthy, and Meese and Deaver joined them in that opinion. The long knives were out, and they were never sheathed after the secretary's faux pas at the time of the President's encounter with a would-be assassin.

Haig was the first "fall guy" in the Reagan administration. He fell because the White House gang distrusted him; they placed every obstacle in his path, and watched him cavort, increasingly barred from White House secret information loops, which they controlled. It was not because they made policy that he was shunted aside; there *was* no policy, at least none in foreign affairs. The conditions in the White House guaranteed that there would be none.

Ronald Reagan believed in the conventional pieties; he did not imagine himself an intellectual, and did not see himself as a professional politician who arrived with a foreign policy agenda. He was, in his romantic imagination, a rancher and a businessman. That, in any case, was how he wished to be viewed, if the 1976 bicentennial edition of *Who's Who in America* was to be believed. He came to the White House because he and his wife wished to live there. Even had he never been wounded—had he not been required to undergo major surgery in 1985 and again in 1987—indolence and disengagement would still have been his characteristic attitudes. Incapable of —and indifferent to—learning what he needed to know to conduct complex international negotiations, having no comprehension of the nuances of foreign policy, he preferred to treat diplomacy as theater, mixing with those who accepted him for what he was, President of the United States and an excellent raconteur.

Secretary Haig, as the disciple of Kissinger, imagined that he, too, might further the "peace process," resolving certain long-standing Arab-Israeli tensions, ameliorating the lot of the Palestinians. It was all an illusion. With Iran no longer in the American camp—the Ayatollah Khomeini having managed to do to the United States what Anwar el-Sadat had done to the Soviet Union a decade earlier, break an alliance based largely on arms sales and a presumed identity of geopolitical interests—the United States was on the lookout for new Gulf allies. Given the political and military instabilities in the region, Saudi Arabia seemed the most eligible candidate for the role. In his last months in office, President Carter had set that courtship in motion, offering the Saudi king the one precious commodity the Americans could supply in abundance—modern arms.

President Reagan expected to fulfill those engagements, clearly in the country's national interest. The Americans knew that the way to the Saudi heart (and purse) was through the sale of highly sophisticated weapons. The Vice President, during the time the President was indisposed recovering from his gunshot wound, advanced the plan to sell AWACS—the system promised the Saudis—recognizing its commercial and diplomatic value. While Secretary Haig thought principally in geopolitical terms, the Vice President thought as a man of business who knew the Middle Eastern mecca of oil. In this instance, they reached the same conclusion—Saudi Arabia ought to be sold AWACS; the Senate ought to be persuaded to approve the deal. Israel's opposition to it was unreasonable, in any case secondary.

If the Secretary of State was correct that the Saudis, increasingly troubled by terrorism, Islamic fundamentalism, and Soviet penetration of the region, ardently wished to improve their relations with the United States, this was a golden opportunity for the new administration. The Vice President, told that the Iranian revolution was on the verge of collapse—one of the fixed orthodoxies of the Reagan years—agreed that collaboration with moderate Arab states like Kuwait and Saudi Arabia was the way into the Arab world. Friendship with them carried the promise of many dividends, not the least being a willingness on their part, in time, to forgive Sadat's Egypt for its "crime" of having made peace with Israel. With these major Arab states in line, Soviet influence in the region would be reduced, and, more importantly, Israel would be compelled to negotiate seriously, returning land for peace. The Middle East, under American guidance, would become a tranquil world.

It was an idyllic picture, wholly ignoring the nature of both Arab and Israeli grievances. While the Secretary of State dwelled on the instabilities in the region—Saudi Arabia and the oil sheikdoms surrounded by unfriendly and unstable neighbors; Iraq and Iran engaged in a bloody war; the Soviet Union's large and continuing influence in Syria; the civil war in Lebanon, with the PLO a "state within a state" in that once prosperous republic; Egypt, a pariah for all other Arabs—the AWACS sale was expected to be a breakthrough in U.S. relations with the moderate states of the Arab world. Rarely had so much been anticipated from an arms sale. Still, there were reasons for the secretary's confidence. He accepted the geopolitical wisdom of Sadat, who saw the Soviet Union as pursuing a "two-crescents policy" in the Middle East and Africa, with the first running through Iraq, Syria, the Yemens, Somalia, and Ethiopia, and the second organized in southern Africa, principally in the former Portuguese colonies. The Soviet objective, according to Sadat, was to cut Africa in two, isolating moderate Arab regimes like his own, increasingly vulnerable to Libyan and PLO terror. The United States had no alternative but to extend protection.

The Secretary of State, writing about AWACS years later, acknowledged that the anticipated $8.5 billion sale, and the benefits it would provide both American industry and labor, weighed heavily with the National Security Council. The great question, however, was whether the Senate would understand the matter, whether its pro-Israel members would seek to thwart the administration in its efforts. By law, any such sale could be nullified if a majority in both houses of Congress refused to approve it. If, however, one house recommended cancellation and the other accepted, the deal could go forward. In the House, with its large Democratic majority, the President could not hope to win; in the Senate, where the Republicans had a small majority, victory was certainly possible. The National Security Council, on April 1, 1981, with Vice President Bush in the chair—the President being in the hospital—voted to approve the decision to sell the Saudis enhanced F-15s and the AWACS. The next task was to win a favorable vote in the Senate.

While the Reagan administration was preoccupied with these issues, Israel, on June 7, to the astonishment and dismay of many in the United States and abroad, bombed and destroyed Iraq's Osirak nuclear reactor, located about ten miles outside Baghdad. In the months that followed, the Israelis repeatedly engaged in military operations intended to diminish PLO influence in Lebanon, to halt attacks launched from that country on Israeli settlements. The administration fretted, admonished, and achieved almost nothing. Continuing with his campaign to secure Senate approval of the AWACS sale, hoping to alter the political equation in the region, the President, like certain of his Republican predecessors, hoped to withstand the pressure of the Israeli lobby, the Republican Party being less dependent on the Jewish vote than the Democratic Party. On October 29, the President's will was done; the motion to prohibit the sale was defeated in the Senate by a vote of 52–48.

While the Secretary of State reveled in the victory, he knew it to be one of less than cosmic importance. It had in fact been something of a tempest in a teapot, having consumed the time of purportedly busy men. The whole episode, painful to the Israelis, for obvious reasons, was also embarrassing to the Saudis, who did not greatly appreciate Senate questioning of their trustworthiness and reliability. Haig, rather ominously, spoke principally of American-Israeli future relations, of which he said: "I fear our old friendship and our shared values and mingled history will be more severely tested than ever they were on Capitol Hill." What was Haig, years after the event, saying? As usual, discretion was his characteristic valor. The Vice President said nothing, wrote nothing, but clearly took pleasure in having helped the President secure a favorable Senate vote.

Such victories scarcely concealed the fact that the Reagan

administration lacked a viable foreign policy for the Middle East. The President knew nothing of the area; neither he nor his Secretary of State could devise a plan for peace in the region, not least because they perpetually overestimated United States influence. Neither the Arabs nor the Israelis were as malleable as they would have wished them to be. Worse, anti-Arab sentiment, independently of professed pro-Israeli feelings, constantly intruded. The Saudis, for example, were not much liked by Americans who gave any thought to them. Known to be opulent, believed to be dissolute, thought to be hypocrites who pretended to be warriors when they were in fact merchants, good customers for American exports, they could never be considered a serious military threat to anyone, despite their vaunted air power. All this was part of a larger American disdain for the Middle East generally, and more specifically for those who embraced the Islamic faith, veiled their women, tolerated dictatorship, and imagined that modernity consisted of building roads and bridges, creating air forces and tank battalions, and accumulating other high-tech weapons of war.

As Secretary of State, Haig was thwarted not by others with a different foreign policy but by there being none. The Vice President only occasionally figured in the secretary's account of his White House struggles, mostly as one of those who did not fully understand his remarkable designs. Indeed, insofar as any existed that was at all recognizable, it involved the sale of arms. In the Reagan years, American credits and arms sales to Egypt skyrocketed. Saudi Arabia, once Egypt's banker, paying for its expensive arms purchases in the common Arab struggle against Zionism, resigned from that role when Egypt signed the Camp David accords. The United States assumed the role of principal banker and arms supplier. While Israel cared not at all for these arrangements, it could do nothing to oppose sales to an Arab country, itself ostracized, whose enemies included Libya, Syria, and Iraq, all radical Arab states supported by the Soviet Union. American policy after 1981 was to supply Egypt with modern arms, hoping to retain its friendship, believing that in time the traditional relations of amity between Egypt and Saudi Arabia would be restored.

In these circumstances, the Iraq-Iran war scarcely figured in administration thinking. Indeed, there was a remarkable co-incidence between the attitudes of the United States and Israel toward that war. Both were delighted to see two rogue states fight it out. Israel, Saudi Arabia, Jordan, Egypt, and Lebanon preoccupied Washington; keeping the peace between Israel and the forces fighting in Lebanon proved a herculean task, exceeding by far the intellectual capacities and experience of men who little understood the dynamics of a conflict that involved Syria and the PLO, Lebanese Muslims and Christians, Israel, and, only very incidentally, the Soviet Union. Israel, the greatest of the administration's problems, constantly failed to perform in the way Washington would have had it do. Despite frequent warnings to desist from moving into Lebanon, Israel launched a major offensive, purportedly to achieve two pur-poses: to bring an end to the bombardment of Israeli settle-ments by Palestinians and to humiliate and shatter the PLO. The Israeli attack, which began on June 6, 1982, opened with spectacular successes. The Syrian Air Force was shattered; Syria's armies were beaten; the PLO was virtually destroyed, with only defeated remnants remaining entrenched in Beirut. This, in fact, was only the beginning.

Syria's folly in deciding to move additional troops into Lebanon only confirmed the Israeli Prime Minister in his resolve to remove Syria's SAM-6 missiles from their Bekaa Valley emplacements. Within hours of threatening the Syrians, the Israelis attacked again, destroying all the missiles and downing twenty-three additional Syrian aircraft. The Israelis returned to their bases having lost not a single plane of their own. Syria and the PLO had been decisively defeated. The Syrians, blaming the Soviets for sending inferior aircraft, were unable otherwise to explain how they had managed to lose eighty-seven planes without the Israelis losing one. The Secretary of State imagined the moment could not be more propitious for the Syrians and the Israelis to leave Lebanon, for the PLO to leave Beirut. In the end, he failed in his principal objectives. While the Vice President figured among those who again misunderstood his complex strategy, the facts were otherwise. There was never any possibility of the United States achieving with Syria or Israel what it intended; nor, for that matter, was the secretary's apologia for his forced resignation very convincing. The story was simple; the President lacked a Middle East policy and was scarcely aware of it. He craved harmony in his official family, among his docile subordinates, including the Vice President. Haig had persisted in threatening that harmony.

Within two months of Haig's departure, with George Shultz as the new Secretary of State, the President delivered a major address on Middle Eastern affairs, his first since coming to the White House. Properly billed, and given appropriate publicity, it was intended to move the peace process forward, to create a confederation, joining Palestinians with Jordan. The scheme fell to the ground within months of its inception. The idea that foreign troops would withdraw from Lebanon was wishful thinking. Syria, though defeated in combat, quickly recovered its military strength. Massive arms shipments, including tanks and advanced fighter aircraft, estimated to be worth more than $2.5 billion, arrived from the Soviet Union and exceeded by far the losses Syria suffered during the fighting with Israel. The king of Jordan, on whom the President relied, was disappointed that neither the Syrians nor the Israelis left Lebanon, that the PLO Executive Committee would not agree to the arrangement he had worked out for a Palestinian negotiating team. Worse, from his point of view, was Syria's new domination of the so-called anti-Arafat PLO terrorists, led by Abu Nidal. The Syrians, allied with forces uninterested in the American peace plan, renewed and expanded their attacks on Israel, and Menachem Begin went forward to plan yet new settlements on the West Bank.

As the world watched, the Lebanon situation deteriorated steadily. American goodwill, a commodity of no great value, counted for nothing. The President's capacity to move Israel proved minimal; even less successful with Syria, not surprisingly, given the Soviet Union's influence there, he turned to domestic issues, to be brought back to the Middle East by a new tragedy. While the American Marines, originally sent into Lebanon in August 1982, along with French and Italian forces, to guarantee the withdrawal of the PLO forces from Beirut, had been withdrawn soon after the President's speech of September 1, they were not absent for very long. Bashir Gemayel, the Phalangist leader, elected President of Lebanon on August 23, 1982, with Israel's support, was assassinated three weeks later. Israeli troops moved immediately into West Beirut, having previously promised the Americans not to do so. In a secret order issued by Israel's General Staff, Israeli troops were explicitly forbidden to enter the Sabra and Shatila refugee camps, believed to contain PLO guerrilla remnants. The order read: "Searching and mopping up the camps will be done by the Phalangists and the Lebanese Army." Days later, the Phalangists did precisely that, shocking the world by massacring hundreds of people, including innocent men, women, and children.

Following these events, the new Lebanese President urgently requested the immediate return of the United States Marines. President Reagan agreed to send them, but for a short time only; they would go as a peacekeeping team, and not engage in combat. Their sole purpose, the President explained to Congress, was to help Lebanon and the Lebanese Army maintain the territorial integrity and political independence of the country. The Marines, he said, would act as a "presence," to support the Lebanese central authority; for a few months, they helped create some semblance of order in the country. In March 1983, that era came to an abrupt end. Five Marines suffered injury in a terrorist attack. A month later, a suicide bomber drove his Chevrolet pickup truck into the American Embassy building in Beirut, killing sixty. The Syrians, increasingly belligerent, armed their supporters in Lebanon and the country seemed again on the verge of civil war. On August 29, two U.S. Marines were killed and fourteen others wounded in a battle between the Lebanese Army and their Muslim foes. On September 1, a year after he made his original plea for peace in the Middle East, the President ordered an additional 2,000 Marines into the Mediterranean, in the waters outside Beirut.

On September 16, Arafat returned secretly to Lebanon. The next day, American naval forces bombarded Syrian-controlled positions in Lebanon. Syria warned the United States that it would retaliate if the attacks continued. By September 19, Druze positions in the hills around Beirut were being systematically shelled by the U.S. Navy. The White House insisted that the safety of the American forces in Lebanon required the action. France, critical of these operations, counseled against them, but to no avail. The President knew that they carried no risk, nothing comparable to a ground campaign, where the possibility of a significant number of American casualties deterred him. In the circumstances, Congress saw no reason to complain.

The situation was wholly changed a month later, on October 23, 1983, just after dawn, when 241 American servicemen were killed in a suicide bombing attack on a Marine barracks in Beirut. An attack at almost the same time on a French military installation left fifty-nine dead. The United States had eyes only for its own tragic loss. The President termed the attack "vicious and cowardly," and vowed that the Americans would not be driven from Beirut. Again, he was posturing. The Syrians became more active than ever in Lebanon; Arafat established headquarters in downtown Beirut and promised to "fight to the end." On November 4, in an attack closely resembling that on the Marine barracks, the Israeli headquarters in Tyre was destroyed by Palestinians, with sixty Israeli dead and thirty wounded. The Israelis retaliated immediately, striking at Palestinian positions in the mountains surrounding Beirut.

Late in November, the new Israeli Prime Minister, Itzhak Shamir, met with the President in Washington; the two announced that they were establishing a joint committee to coordinate military activities. A few days later, planes from American carriers attacked Syrian positions in Lebanon, in response to Syrian attacks on unarmed American reconnaissance airplanes. Two American planes were shot down and one American pilot was captured by the Syrians. Syria reported two dead and ten wounded in the American attack. That same day, eight American Marines died from artillery fire of Syrian-backed Druze militia outside Beirut. The United States continued its bombardments from the sea, much preferring such a military response to any that might involve land combat, with the prospect of large numbers of Marine casualties. Syrian and Druze positions were attacked by the powerful guns of the battleship *New Jersey*, and great damage was thought to have been done.

The President, increasingly pressed by members of the Cabinet and certain of his White House colleagues, heard new arguments for the rapid removal of the Marines from Lebanon. A second disaster comparable to that of October 23 could only create political problems for him. The elections were looming; November 1984 was more important than anything that might be gained by keeping the Marines in Lebanon. The President saw no reason to resist the advice proffered, preferring it to that offered by his Secretary of State, who believed that the Marines should stay, that their sudden departure would only damage United States credibility in the Middle East. Reagan's second Secretary of State, like his first, did not understand the President's political calculus. A foreign disaster could make a great difference in the election, and thus, with no Middle East victory in sight, Lebanon became an inconsequential pawn. It would simply have to take care of itself. In a year, it was no more stable than it had been the day the Americans first intervened.

The initiative of September 1982 led to nothing. It involved the Americans in difficulties with the Israelis, and demonstrated to the Jordanians, again, American impotence in the face of Arab and Israeli intransigence. It revealed the limits of the President's resolve. Prepared to engage in military operations with obviously inferior powers, he had no concept of larger strategic objectives. The President knew the Middle East not at all. No one in his immediate entourage understood its tragic complexities.

Insofar as the Reagan administration may be said to have had any consistent policy in the Middle East, apart from the fact that it intervened lightheartedly in Lebanon and fled ignominiously the moment the heat was turned on, that policy involved almost indiscriminate sales of arms to Saudi Arabia and Egypt, Israel, Lebanon, and Jordan, and more secretly and more sporadically to Iraq and Iran. The last created the most serious of the scandals of Reagan's second term. Though the "arms-for-hostages deal" was a shocking and cynical assault on the democratic process, it served mostly to withdraw public and media attention from substantially more serious foreign policy flaws. The United States never developed a policy with respect to the Iraq-Iran war, and never imagined it needed to have one. It intervened militarily in Lebanon, but believed it could do so without risk. It used its navy to lob shells into fixed Arab positions, knowing there was no possibility of effective reprisal. In this, as in so much else, the President sought to conduct foreign policy on the cheap, without political costs. It did not work, either with Arabs or with others, and almost no

one said so, failing to recognize its moral obliquity. The United
States, led by men with no notion of ethical obligation, acted
impetuously and imperiously.

Because the geopolitical situation in the Middle East had
changed with the expulsion of the Shah, what made American
policy under Reagan so irrelevant was that it became fixated
in his second term on a single problem—the American hostages
taken by Shiites in Lebanon, thought to be collaborating closely
with revolutionary colleagues in Iran. For the President, the
great offense was not that a fanatic in Teheran threatened the
Gulf and might one day endanger Saudi Arabia and other
Middle Eastern monarchies, but that Iran had become the
chief supporter of Shiite terrorism in Lebanon, where American civilians were being seized and held, tortured and killed.

In his second term, the President saw the hostage crisis as
the all-important one; it consumed what little attention he had
to spare for such matters. No one, least of all the Vice President,
sought to instruct him about it. Though the President thundered and raged, he was as impotent in liberating the few
Americans taken in Beirut as his predecessor had been in
freeing the many taken in Teheran. The hostage issue became
one the United States itself became hostage to, and no one
more than the President himself. This was an issue he could
understand and relate to. Like Henry II begging for someone
to rid him of his cursed archbishop, Reagan, a less violent man,
must have frequently expressed the wish that his government
might be spared further humiliation at the hands of religious
and political fanatics. One cannot imagine the President using
historical parallels—they did not exist for him—but he knew
that the Carter solution, the sending of a military force to free
hostages, was not one he cared to repeat.

In the end, those who advised him recommended the use of
the only resource which seemed to move Middle Eastern
governments—the sale of arms. When all else failed—diplomacy having been an inadequate policy resource throughout

the Reagan years—his men turned to the sale of arms, believing they might be used to accelerate the return of the kidnapped hostages. The President's second term was a fitting epilogue to the first; it showed the same lack of imagination, of serious dialogue within the government, between the executive and Congress, the President and the American people. Irangate was more than a "covert operation"; it was the ultimate gulling of the nation, achieved through deceit. The Vice President knew about it; he knew also that he would not be caught out, because the public, accustomed to the President's rhetoric, believed him. They could not imagine that so principled a man was lying, brazenly and consistently.

The November 1984 elections had been a "cakewalk" for the President, requiring slight effort and no defense of failures to achieve a promised balanced budget in his third year and an anticipated surplus in the fourth. All that had been forgotten. The early polls, taken soon after his renomination at the Republican Party's Dallas convention, told his managers that the election would be a romp. The President, appearing before 17,000 Republican faithful at a prayer breakfast, intoned on his favorite theme: politics and morality were inseparable. Believing in God, the President never alluded to his own mortality. That was a forbidden subject. While Dwight Eisenhower hesitated before agreeing to run for a second term, knowing the state of his health, wondering whether he would survive the ordeal of another four years in the White House, and questioning the wisdom of having Richard Nixon renominated as Vice President, such issues never existed for Ronald Reagan about himself or his putative successor. Taking sustenance from the adulation of crowds who attended his every public sortie, he enjoyed a national regard that derived neither from his grasp of complex domestic and international issues nor from his close personal friendship with prominent fellow Republicans. The Vice President marveled at his success.

The President's principal friend abroad, in a class by herself, without rival, was of course Margaret Thatcher. It was one of the more honest of the President's relations, though it never led to foreign policy innovations of any consequence or even major corrections of course. Prime Minister Thatcher, like so many others, indulged her American friend. Each served the other's purposes. After her Falklands victory, the President, on his way to Versailles to attend an economic summit, stopped in London to honor his friend. Appearing before a joint session of the two houses of Parliament, he lauded Mrs. Thatcher for her "ability at decision-making and firm action." The greatest honor, however, he reserved for the brave men who fought, freedom fighters all, who battled not for material gain, to win "mere real estate," but to uphold principle. They knew, as did their Prime Minister, that they fought for a cause, "for the belief that armed aggression must not be allowed to succeed."

Given such Anglo-American friendship and mutual esteem, small quarrels remained minor squalls, storms that lasted a day or a week, were quickly over, and left no damage. Indeed, the President, in the Prime Minister's mind, could do no wrong; the sentiment was reciprocated. Still, there were occasional quarrels, misunderstandings, as with Grenada, a tiny Caribbean island, a member of the Commonwealth, that had fallen under the influence of a small Marxist clique. When its Prime Minister, Maurice Bishop, a protégé of Fidel Castro, was assassinated, there was concern that law and order were threatened, that the 800 Americans on the island might be in danger. Neighboring Caribbean states, anxious for the safety of their own regimes, urged the British and the Americans to intervene, to restore order. The British gave no attention to these requests. The Reagan White House, however, took them more seriously; believing the threat to be real, they decided to intervene, without consulting the British or the United States Congress. Both would be told when the "rescue" was underway. A small American task force was assembled and moved rapidly to achieve its mission, the restoration of peace in the threatened region.

The American aggression was deliberate, legitimated with the fig leaf of a specific request for help from the so-called Organization of Eastern Caribbean States. The war merited a musical comedy motif, but Margaret Thatcher refused to regard it in that light. Furious, she demanded an explanation from her American friend. The President explained that he would have consulted with the British had he not feared that his secret invasion plans would be leaked. He never made wholly explicit whether he feared a leak in London or in Washington. In his simple anti-Communism, the President could not believe that his motives for going into Grenada could be questioned. Mrs. Thatcher, while disinclined to make too public her disappointment with him, remarked in a BBC World Service broadcast: "Many peoples in many countries would love to be free of Communism, but that doesn't mean to say we can just walk into them and say now you are free." Between the President's anti-Communism and that of the British Conservative Party leader, a gulf existed. Nevertheless, Margaret Thatcher had no reason to dwell on the subject; she refused to say anything that might prove embarrassing to the President in the months immediately preceding his campaign for reelection.

Nor did she or other members of her government think to dispute or correct the highly romantic accounts the President delivered on the "magnificently successful" Grenada operation. Not only did he wildly exaggerate the power of the "enemy" forces the Americans encountered while persistently understating the number of American casualties suffered through "friendly fire," but he totally misrepresented the issues. In his account of the operation's progress, as given in his autobiography, it all began with a 4 a.m. meeting at the Augusta National Golf Course, where Bud McFarlane, four days into his job as National Security Adviser, summoned him to meet with the Secretary of State, to discuss, via a secure telephone line with George Bush, serving in his absence as head of the White House crisis management team, a very grave situation that had developed during the night.

"In robe and pajamas," Reagan listened to an account of Grenada's Cuban-supported "military buildup," thought to be preparatory to an invasion of Jamaica, Barbados, St. Vincent's, St. Lucia, Dominica, and Antigua. All six wanted to resist; none had the military capability to do so. They were appealing for American help, and the President recognized how difficult it was to turn them away. Also, with 800 American students in Grenada attending medical school—in the President's words, "all of them potential hostages"—he asked how quickly a "rescue commission" could be mobilized and dispatched. The Joint Chiefs believed it could be done in forty-eight hours. The President said: "Do it." The "rescue mission"—a wonderful phrase, worthy of an accomplished wordsmith—came into being, and the President went back to bed. Providing additional details, he explained why he wished for the operation to be kept secret. Congress, still suffering from its "post-Vietnam syndrome," should not be allowed to intervene, impeding an essential mission. The President knew that if he gave Congress notice, many would argue that the country was letting itself in for "another Vietnam." Grenada was the President's decision, his war, made with the advice and consent of the Vice President and the Secretary of State, if not of the United States Congress—which, as any good Republican knew, could not be trusted.

Such foreign policy and military concerns preoccupied the President in his first term. What, then, preoccupied him and his new White House staff—he lost both Baker and Meese to major Cabinet positions, but of course kept faithful Bush as Vice President—during the second term? They were matters that derived their significance mostly from the extent of the media publicity that could be milked from them. Terrorism

and Central America were the President's major preoccupa-
tions; he saw Iran and Nicaragua as members of "a new
international version of Murder, Incorporated," linked with
Libya, North Korea, and Cuba, all described as "outlaw states
run by the strangest collection of misfits, Looney Tunes, and
squalid criminals since the advent of the Third Reich."

The President, preoccupied with these matters and more
generally with Communist infiltration in Central and South
America, lost no sleep in pondering the complexities of the
Iran-Iraq war, reflecting on how that conflict might be resolved,
perhaps to the advantage of the United States. Indeed, his
interest in Iran dwelled principally on its image as the quintessential radical terrorist state, intent on creating havoc in the
world. The implications of the Iran-Iraq war, for the belligerents, for the other Gulf states, and for security more generally
in the Middle East figured only spasmodically. After the
proliferation of Shiite kidnappings of Americans in Beirut—
three taken hostage in 1984, four in 1985—the President
dwelled increasingly on that single issue. Many recommendations were offered, including secret negotiations with the kid-
nappers. The President would not hear of it, at least if his
public statements could be believed. On June 30, 1985, a few
weeks before he entered the hospital for the removal of a large
intestinal polyp, he said: "The United States gives terrorists no
rewards. We make no concessions. We make no deals."

Increasingly attentive to the situation, but having no thoughts
on how to resolve it, he listened on his return from the hospital
to discussions in the National Security Council on a post-
Khomeini Iran. The Ayatollah Khomeini's demise was thought
to be imminent; it was natural that the NSC should wish to
consider how the United States might profit from the change,
perhaps influencing Iranian developments. The capacity of the
United States to deceive itself about what it could do in the
Middle East was immense. These events coincided with others,
equally secret at the time, and subsequently revealed, that led

the NSC under McFarlane's direction, to consider various American arms-sales initiatives. After the Irangate affair became public, and particularly after the publication of the Tower Commission report—a purportedly objective study of the whole abortive operation—the American public learned how Israel sought to use the United States for its purposes, how the President used the Israelis, how both deceived the Iranians, and were in turn deceived by them, and how the whole illegal use of profits from the sale of arms to Iran was intended to help the Contras, against the explicit will of Congress, and without its knowledge. It was a tale of chicanery at every level.

On August 6, 1985, at the White House, in his private quarters, a recuperating President met with his principal advisers, including the Vice President, the Secretary of State, the Secretary of Defense, the White House Chief of Staff, Donald Regan, and the National Security Adviser, at that time McFarlane, to discuss the request "pro-American" Iranians were making for a dialogue with the United States, which was expected to show its goodwill by agreeing to a sale of arms. George Shultz, in his version of the meeting, recalled that both he and Secretary Weinberger opposed the proposition, believing it wrong to fall into "the arms-for-hostages business." The President himself appeared undecided about the matter and said little. Shultz recalled that the President "didn't seem to push one way or the other. He listened and it seemed to be relatively new information for him." McFarlane, believing the President had already approved of the deal, represented his concern as being principally that the arms go only to Iranians opposed to Khomeini's policies. No one kept minutes of the meeting. Indeed, no one asked who the "good Iranians" were or why they should have an interest in seeking to accommodate the Americans. In any case, it was taken for granted that Israel would ship the arms, thereby helping to liberate the hostages. No one recalled whether the Vice President said anything.

In the months that followed, two things became clear: arms

were being shipped to Iran through Israel; they were not going to some "dissident or opposition faction," as McFarlane maintained, but to the Iranian government. Another Chief Executive might have considered that the time had come to halt the operation. Information provided him had been false; the Americans were secretly supplying arms to one of the belligerents in the Iraq-Iran war, a declared enemy of the United States. On January 7, 1986, at a meeting of the National Security Council, with the Secretary of State and the Secretary of Defense expressing their opposition to the plan to exchange arms for hostages, and the National Security Adviser and the Director of the CIA expressing approval, the President listened and said little. William Casey argued that the prospect of an intelligence gain justified the whole operation. Shultz said, much later: "Well, it seemed to me that as people around the room talked, Secretary Weinberger and I were the only ones who were against it. And so that included everybody who was there on the other side of the issue, which surprised me, and it almost seemed unreal, and I couldn't believe that people would want to do this. I thought it was a bad idea." No one remembered what the Vice President said, but he was not among those who questioned the sales' propriety or necessity.

A major covert operation was undertaken, with the approval of the President and the CIA, against the opposition of the heads of State and Defense. The new National Security Adviser, Admiral John M. Poindexter, abetted by his subordinate, Lieutenant Colonel Oliver L. North, and in cooperation with the CIA, arranged the details of the transfer of arms. Because the United States might expect a certain profit from the sales, North, anxious always to please the President, began to entertain an idea that grew increasingly attractive to him. Why not divert some of the profits from the arms sales to Iran to support the Contra "freedom fighters" in Nicaragua? The Democratic Congress, hostile to the Contras, had refused to vote the appropriations recommended by the President. Why not con-

coct a scheme to achieve that purpose secretly? To help
Nicaragua's "freedom fighters" was to fight Communism, to
do what was also being done in Iran. What better or more
appropriate use could be made of the anticipated arms-sales
profits? As he would proudly testify later, North thought it a
"neat idea," and had no difficulty persuading his chief, Admiral
Poindexter, of its merits. The Iran-Contra connection was
born. The architects of the policy, a tiny group in the White
House, in constant touch with the Director of the CIA, took
for granted that they were doing what the President wanted.

What began so modestly as a secret effort to supply unnamed
friendly Iranians with arms, theoretically to assist them in the
succession battle that would follow on the Ayatollah's death,
ended with revelations about arms sales to the Iranian government as a way of liberating American hostages, with the profit
from the sales going to private individuals, and the greater
part to the Contras, "freedom fighters" whom the Congress of
the United States firmly refused to sustain.

When the American press turned up its first evidence on the
matter, the story was wholly about Nicaragua, but the Iran
connection was soon discovered and disclosed. The game, so
secretly and ineffectively played, with its comic cast of "true
believers" pretending to professional competence as intelligence experts, all the while prevaricating and inventing, was
almost crafted for television coverage. Each day brought its
new disclosures, and the plot, as it unfolded, threatened to
become television's soap opera of the season. The responsibility
of American journalism precluded its becoming that. Indeed,
the moral of Irangate was never fully explored. The blame lay
wholly with an incompetent President, who knew nothing about
foreign policy, was badly served by those, including the Vice
President, who never dared instruct him, and who in fact knew
little more. His Secretary of State, George Shultz, an academic
and corporate executive of considerable intellect who enjoyed
the perquisites of his office, was never able to win the President's

confidence, to become either a confidant or a spokesman, to impose himself, to be candid about what he knew or thought. Never gaining the President's ear, he was unable to influence him. Had he done so, certain of the Iran-Contra inanities would not have occurred. If the Vice President ever said anything to suggest that the whole operation was illegal, no one heard him.

The President's concern was wholly with international terrorism, perpetrated by men and women supported by foul dictators, whose violent acts led to the murder of innocent Americans. When he was not reflecting on hostages in Lebanon—a major and continuing worry, and one which the British Prime Minister seemed never able wholly to share—he fretted about the new evidences of terrorism elsewhere. Attacks in the Rome and Vienna airports during the 1985 Christmas holidays killed nineteen men and women, of whom five were American citizens. It was widely believed that the Libyan government, on the orders of its President, Muammar al-Qaddafi, financed and masterminded these attacks. The Libyans, realizing that the Americans might be preparing an air strike against them, warned that if the United States bombed Libya, all Western European cities would become vulnerable to retaliatory action. President Reagan, searching for NATO support to halt Libya's terrorism, initiated discussions that considered various possibilities: an economic boycott of Libya; the introduction of sanctions.

Margaret Thatcher, questioning the efficacy of these proposals, objected even more strenuously to a military solution, arguing quite simply: "I do not believe in retaliatory strikes that are against international law." Still, after learning of another Libyan terrorist attack in April, this time in Berlin, she knew what to expect. The President intended an air strike—a safe military action—against Libya. When he asked to use the American F-111 bombers stationed in Britain, part of NATO's deterrent force against Soviet aggression in Europe, for his Libyan operation, the Prime Minister agreed, despite strenuous objections from certain of her colleagues. Her friendship with the President was too important to allow ethical or political convictions of individual ministers to take precedence. While some in Britain thought the American bombings barbaric, and criticized the President for what he did, Margaret Thatcher was not among them. She, like those who served him in the White House, knew better than to question his actions, always represented as both moral and necessary. Besides, the operation proved to be cheap in terms of the only measure the White House used—American lives lost.

Ronald Reagan, almost always lucky, never experienced the blows that might have befallen him given his feckless pursuit of an old man's comfort and ease. Just as he came to the White House an innocent in matters of foreign policy, he left in almost precisely the same condition. In his neglect of the subject—and indeed in his failure to give authority to others who might have initiated lawful diplomatic initiatives—he helped corrupt the policymaking system. Instinctively, those who worked closely with him became courtiers, silent in their opposition, if they ever thought to disagree with actions taken in his name. In addressing larger purposes in the area of foreign policy, and not only in the Middle East, few initiatives were taken.

The President taught his "team" a simple lesson—the American public, generous and uncritical, would be indulgent toward those who lived at 1600 Pennsylvania Avenue only if their pocketbooks were full and if the "wars" waged in their name were undertaken always against "wimps," foreign leaders whose verbal strength greatly exceeded their military capability. One other lesson was paramount: the American public had little memory and placed no great store on that faculty. In short, sufficient to the day was the President's concern with the news clips that appeared nightly, that emphasized his courage and determination to rebuild America's defenses, all in the cause of world peace.

The President was an incomparable storyteller; he was an even more accomplished mythmaker. While Margaret Thatcher might be a delightful social companion, a kindred soul, another self-made person committed to the same conservative values he espoused, she could never create the "story line" he wanted for the history books. She could never do for the "Gipper" what Mikhail Gorbachev could do. In the President's second term, Gorbachev became the principal player in a drama, better described as a fiction, that the President invented and used to conceal something more important than the Iran-Contra debacle—his failure to lead the nation in the moral regeneration he constantly called for.

Reagan was the principal architect of his own myth, and he gave its most eloquent statement in his autobiography, *Ronald Reagan: An American Life*. The autobiography opens with an account of the President meeting his Soviet counterpart for the first time in Geneva. This, he tells us, was the day he had been looking forward to for five years; his diary notation the previous evening carried the simple words: "Lord, I hope I'm ready."

The President showed his habitual adroitness in portraying his own ambitions, so obviously transcending those of the men who served him. George Shultz had told him that the summit would be a success if agreement was reached to meet again. He, the President, "wanted to accomplish more than that." Believing in personal relationships, having concluded during his first years in the White House that some people in the Kremlin feared the United States—obviously, without reason —the President arrived with "a plan"; while the diplomats and arms control experts might meet together, the important thing was for him to see Gorbachev alone, to persuade the Soviet leader, so different from his predecessors, that the United States wanted peace. The President's words are worth quoting: "That morning, as we shook hands and I looked into his smile, I sensed I had been right and felt a surge of optimism that my plan might work."

It did; the two, before a blazing hearth, alone with their interpreters, talked. The President began with his accustomed admixture of modesty and hyperbole, born of a lifetime of self-indulgent listening to and repeating American political clichés. He said: "Here you and I are, two men in a room, probably the only two men in the world who could bring about World War III. But by the same token, we may be the only two men in the world who could perhaps bring about peace in the world." How to achieve that noble objective? The mistrust between the Soviet Union and the United States, which had produced the arms race in the first instance, had to be reduced. "Mutual assured destruction"—MAD—was indeed mad. "A button push away from oblivion," the President had already tried to tell the Soviet leader, in one of his letters, that "no one could win a nuclear war," that such a war must never be fought. The possibility that the same message had been delivered by all the President's predecessors, for well over two decades, was inconsequential to the tale the President was weaving. It was his friendship, his closeness to Gorbachev, that caused the thing to happen.

Still, the President could not use his Prologue simply to celebrate the close relationship he established almost immediately with Gorbachev at Geneva. The Geneva summit would not have come about had he not labored so effectively and persistently to rebuild America's defenses. He came to the White House with the American military in a shambles; he had changed it all. And once he did, he knew that the Soviets would appreciate American strength, and would do what he had always wanted them to do, come to the negotiating table.

So his dream was realized. All that talk of the "evil empire," so misunderstood by his political opponents, had concealed his true purpose, to bring the Soviets to want peace as much as he did. This had been his intention from the beginning, but "the Soviet leaders kept dying on me." Finally, meeting with a younger Soviet leader, the President had an opportunity to instruct him. But, according to the Great Communicator, Mikhail Gorbachev, for all his intelligence, knew very little about the United States. Myths had to be discarded if mistrust and misunderstanding were to be cast away. It was important for the Soviet leader to understand that American military technology was now (since 1981) overwhelmingly superior to that of the Soviet Union, that the United States could go on outspending the Soviets if they did not agree to arms reductions. In short, Ronald Reagan said modestly, he told Mikhail Gorbachev that the arms race was one "which I think you know you can't win." He had been blunt; his purpose had been noble; he was striving for peace. Before the morning was over, the two agreed to two additional summits, in Washington and Moscow. Shultz had indeed been too limited in his aim. He lacked a sufficient appreciation of the remarkable talents of his chief.

The President knew that he had not changed; the world had changed, for the better. In the words of his autobiography: "The world was approaching the threshold of a new day. We had a chance to make it a safer, better place for now and the twenty-first century." Dean Acheson might imagine he was "present at the creation"; Franklin Roosevelt died knowing he had all but defeated a dictator who aspired to world domination; President Reagan, unable to make Assad, Qaddafi, or unnamed Communists in Grenada equivalent to Hitler, posed as the great "peacemaker." The role fitted him superbly; he was the star actor; the American people served as the supporting cast. Through the sacrifices of American citizens, who accepted the necessity of an expensive military buildup, and against the persistent objections of ill-informed and hostile Democrats, he caused the Soviet Union to become an economic "basket case," prepared in the end to sue for an ideological and political armistice.

The story was perfect, the apotheosis brilliant. It bore as much relation to the truth as did his account of how, in Moscow, he urged the dismantling of the Berlin Wall, and again in his speech at the Brandenburg Gate, only to see the Wall come down a year and a half later. Who could doubt the connection? Reagan, always modest, never claimed sole credit; he was prepared to share it with the Soviet leader, who, for whatever mysterious reasons, had seen the need to change.

On a pad of paper that bore the printed heading DON'T LET THE TURKEYS GET YOU DOWN, the President left a final message for his successor. Again, it was vintage Reagan. He wrote: "Dear George, You'll have moments when you want to use this particular stationery. Well, go for it. George, I treasure the memories we share and wish you all the very best. You'll be in my prayers. God bless you and Barbara. I'll miss our Thursday lunches. Ron." The President passed on the baton to one he helped train, confident that it would be used for the good of the American people, as he himself had so consistently tried to do, by the only lights he had: memories of an America that had never been, of himself as he never was.

# President Bush: The Apprentice

On January 20, 1989, George Bush became President of the United States. The foolproof Reagan design required him to wrap himself in the American flag and preach homilies, to do little, pretending all the while to be busy bringing America back to its traditional virtuous ways. But the man who had learned so much from his eight years in the White House almost threw away the benefits of that apprenticeship in his first eighteen months in office. Happily for himself, he recouped his losses, and followed his master in a foreign expedition that marked him as a Reagan Republican of the deepest dye. He prepared for and fought a war that was a lark, proved his manhood, and showed himself the true son of the political father who knew that wars ought to be fought against inferiors only: cheaply, quickly, successfully, and always in the name of peace. In the spectacular war President Bush fought and won, not many more Americans lost their lives than those who slept away in the tragic morning hours of a Beirut terror bombing.

Having learned lessons that made him appealing to white males—still a dominant group in the American electorate, if not in the nation—Bush knew little about how to conduct foreign policy if it required leaving the well-worn Cold War paths trod by Nixon and Reagan. Believing that he could enter the Middle East quagmire without danger, creating a useful new alliance with Arab states that would allow him to defeat a vile dictatorship, Iraq, while also pressuring an old ally, Israel, he developed a scenario scarcely different from what his immediate predecessor tried to do. The President, having learned little about the Middle East in his eight years in the White House, appointed a close friend as Secretary of State who knew even less. Both lived with the illusion that new circumstances provided greater opportunity for successful Middle East negotiations. Their friendship with the President of the Soviet Union suggested a new strategy; they would jointly pressure their respective clients, Israelis and Arabs, to make peace, in everyone's interest.

The President exaggerated American power, looked away from American and Soviet weaknesses, and greatly overestimated the benefits of American-Soviet collaboration, particularly in an area like the Middle East. More seriously, perhaps, he ignored how much the situation had changed since the day he traveled to the Capitol to take his oath of office as President. His 1989 Central and Eastern European bounty—a political inheritance he did nothing to create—delighted him, demonstrating the incontestable power of American democracy and the superiority of its market economy. Like Ronald Reagan, he failed to understand the significance of the events that led Gorbachev to experiment with *perestroika* and *glasnost*. Misconstruing America's role in leading the Soviet Union to be more pacific, he ignored the continuing difficulties of a fragile state incapable of coping with a tottering economy. Offered the opportunity to strike out on novel paths, the President had not the faintest notion of what to do. Nothing in his life had prepared him for diplomatic adventure, least of all one that required a major change of course.

George Bush was shaped initially by a too easy existence, a

too conventional upbringing, an insufficient appreciation of the importance of intellect. Later, as an adult, he was too ready to accept ethical expediency, never understanding the deeply corrosive effects of having lived in the service of mean and unethical men. The son of rich, upstanding, conservative Connecticut parents, he made his way in life entirely on his own, but only in his imagination. Bush was sent to the right schools, joined the best clubs, and pursued athletics as avidly as others of his social class did, only to emerge a hollow man, lacking in learning, imagination, and empathy. He lived perpetually, though silently, with a fear of change.

George Bush may best be characterized as a rich late-twentieth-century Republican Party politician who made his way largely through the advantages of inheritance. The Great Inheritor, a Connecticut Yankee masquerading as a self-made Texan, Bush was too well-bred to boast of the precise size of the fortune he acquired during his brief immersion in Texas oil. It certainly gave him the freedom to enjoy advantages appropriate to someone of his social position and political ambition. Unlike other twentieth-century Republican Presidents, including Coolidge, Hoover, Eisenhower, Nixon, and Reagan, Bush did not start at the bottom and make his way up. There was no Abe Lincoln story concealed in the Bush family archives, and even the wish to follow his mentor in fable creation did not allow him to become the all-American boy.

George Bush was the beneficiary of World War II and the Cold War. The child also of a particular social class, identifiably American, which went under the code name of "old money," he started life with many advantages. His tribe was small and isolated, composed of white Anglo-Saxon Protestants of good birth, which translated as men and women of ample inherited income who enjoyed a very special social status in the latter half of the nineteenth and for most of the twentieth century. George Bush entered this privileged world at the moment of his birth in 1924, and never really left it, though his political makeup artists counseled him to avoid too close a public identification with it. While neither Theodore Roosevelt nor William Howard Taft imagined that they lost their political credibility by being known as gentlemen, who belonged to clubs called Porcellian and Skull and Bones, discretion required them not to flaunt such distinctions; it would, in any case, have gone counter to the traditions of their class. Still, they reveled in them, as they did in their respect for learning, love of reading, and impressive, almost effortless articulateness. Bush, though coming from the same class and being able to claim (quietly, of course) the same Skull and Bones connection, lacked the other, more important attributes of his privileged education. He was unlikely to discover them in middle age in the administrations of Richard Nixon and Ronald Reagan.

How was it that he went to an extraordinarily good preparatory school, and then, after distinguished service as a naval officer during World War II, to Yale University, and never emerged with the intellectual curiosity of those of his social class who would have been ashamed to scorn what he so crudely called "that vision thing"? For some of the same reasons that others of his class sometimes exhibited mediocrity, disdained learning, and prided themselves on what they took to be their manliness. But Bush had an even more compelling reason to wish to appear something he was not. He aspired to be a politician in an age when the leader was expected to show the qualities of the larger American tribe, or at least to pretend to have those characteristics. In this, as in so much else, he revealed his contempt for the American people, who did not make toughness the supreme or sole civic virtue.

The WASP aristocracy—unknown to Alexis de Tocqueville, Europe's greatest commentator on early-nineteenth-century America, who insisted that aristocracy in the European sense had no place in the North American world, that the United States boasted only two classes, the rich and the poor—came into its own only after the Civil War. Like so much else in the United States, its life proved to be short. A social class that in its best period founded and sustained learned and philan-thropic institutions, took pride in what it did to create America's reputation as a civilized and public-spirited society committed to the idea of progress and respectful of the importance of tradition, managed to lose much of its self-confident and sometimes exaggerated assertiveness in the drab political cli-mate created by too many post-World War II wars, hot and cold. Bush, as a representative of the class, afraid to show his "patrician" colors, was unwilling even to acknowledge that he knew the meaning of the term. He aspired to be a "good Joe" like so many other Americans and posed as such, though not always convincingly.

In less than half a century, the nation moved from having some sense of moral rectitude to accepting the antics imposed by the Cold War rivalry. When Theodore Roosevelt burst into politics, he claimed that men of his social class founded the Republic, that it was his duty to serve, to remedy abuses and create a new and better America. George Bush simply wanted to be President. How could the decline in ambition be ex-plained? If Bush was a late-twentieth-century representative figure of "old money" America, white men and women who inherited large fortunes acquired in a pre-income tax era in a burgeoning post-Civil War industrial economy, why did he no longer believe in the distinctive culture of his class? Or did he, living it in his private life and simply ignoring it in his public existence? If he still preferred to associate with those of his own kind, seeking privacy in the isolated and socially correct enclaves of Maine, why had he lost a regard for pro bono activities, as exemplified in service on all manner of philan-thropic and cultural boards, signaling a commitment to others less fortunate, less free? More importantly, why had he allowed politics to become his mistress, never realizing either that the association corrupted him or that it need not have done so?

Was the seed of the final corruption planted in the Reagan White House or did it exist earlier, in the time of Nixon? Or did Bush, unwittingly, enjoy all the advantages that attached to wealth and position in the United States and remain conventional because he lacked the historic models that might have pressed him to become something more? Had his privileged family upbringing and schooling, intended to prepare him for a stable world, cast him adrift in one that had become demanding and dangerous, inhospitable to certain kinds of ethical concerns? There was little in his early life to suggest that George Bush was in any way exceptional, though he started with advantages common to boys born of well-to-do parents in Calvin Coolidge's America.

George Bush attended Phillips Andover, one of the more prestigious of America's private schools, which, unlike the "old money" creations of his grandfather's generation, aspired to educate more than the sons of the very rich. To read the Phillips Academy yearbook for 1942, the year George Bush graduated, is to become aware of the ways in which the school's scholarship funds guaranteed a number of places for the sons of parents of limited means, who might then choose to go on to institutions like MIT. Bush showed no interest in things intellectual, but an almost uncanny zest for activity. Doing everything that a well-bred youth in his late teens, accustomed to direction by parents and teachers, could be expected to do, he excelled in sports. The recipient of a John Hopkins Prize, an award "to be divided among those students who have received no demerits, absence or tardy marks, excused or unexcused during the year," he showed himself obedient and responsible.

His extracurricular activity was prodigious. Treasurer and at one time secretary of the Student Council, he served also as an elected member, was president of the senior class for one term, and deputy housemaster. On the Senior Prom Committee, a member of the student newspaper's editorial board for three years, president of the Society of Inquiry, and on the business board of the Academy's yearbook, he not only was captain of soccer, captain of baseball, and manager of basketball, a member of both the JV and varsity baseball teams, the varsity soccer squad, and the varsity basketball team, but managed to find time to serve as student deacon and president of Greeks, the organization that embraced the Academy's "secret societies." The latter, founded late in the nineteenth century, included three of special social distinction, including AUV, to which Bush was, of course, elected. The society's initiation ceremonies, solemn and elaborate, followed the usual adolescent horseplay, with the "scut" taken around town, "forced to stop at some houses and ask for food, to urinate on a few porches, and generally to make a fool of himself."

Bush was not much of a student at the Academy. How could he have been, given his unrivaled participation in every kind of athletic and extracurricular activity? As for an interest in national politics, it figured little in his Andover circle. Still, myth suggests that he was deeply moved by the 1940 commencement address of the Academy's most distinguished living alumnus, Henry Stimson, who delivered the speech only five days before Franklin Roosevelt invited him, a lifelong Republican, to become Secretary of War. Given at a time of great international turmoil, when France was being conquered by Nazi Germany, Stimson's speech invoked a spirit of patriotism and sacrifice, emphasizing principles of trust, fair play, and the traditional Christian respect for the equal value of all human persons.

It is difficult to know whether the speech moved George Bush as deeply as his hagiographers would have us believe, or how it influenced him then or later. Stimson expressed views conventional among those of his social class. George Bush's father, Prescott Bush, who spent almost the whole of his adult life as a partner in Brown Brothers Harriman, would have subscribed to the whole of Stimson's creed. So, also, would others in their social circle in and around New York. When war came to America, men like Prescott Bush rushed to do the pro bono work they thought mandatory. Prescott Bush served first as national campaign manager for the USO, and later as campaign chairman of the National War Fund. After victory, when he was almost sixty, he entered the Senate, representing Connecticut. This commitment to "service," so characteristic of his class and generation, so important to their self-esteem, did not translate simply as a "will to power"; it had more authentically American moral and social roots.

George Bush, a second son, could not fail to please such a father, who may have even believed that the boy would follow in his footsteps. The beginnings were certainly auspicious. As a youth, he excelled in sports; during school holidays, he met at home in Greenwich, Connecticut, others groomed in the same manner, instructed in the same values. In the summer, like other male scions of his social class, he went off for an obligatory vacation, which gave him experience of sailing, intended not so much to hone his already vaunted athletic skills as to give him an experience of the sea and its hazards. Maine, for such privileged families, was more than a summer resort; it allowed them to spend time together, enjoying the many-generational companionship denied the young by an educational system that required wellborn boys of East Coast origins to be sent away to boarding schools and then to Ivy League colleges. For the Bush family, Kennebunkport represented the summer idyll, where boys and girls met others of their sort. The late Victorian American world of the rich, with its very specific rituals, was being perpetuated in a society where privacy and isolation provided social protection.

It was a privileged life, disciplined and regulated, which segregated small numbers of white, Protestant affluent children from others of ethnic, religious, racial, and social origins thought to be inferior. Providing security from a vulgarity known to exist outside, which could be especially dangerous to

impressionable adolescents, it superficially copied certain traditions common among the English upper classes. There was
never any intention, however, in the fashion of certain Victorian
public (i.e., private) schools to raise up a generation of "gentlemen," committed to public service in a military or civilian
capacity. The privileged social enclaves of early-twentieth-
century America, including its schools, existed to make the
sons of the rich comfortable among their own, creating personal
links—the word "connections" was much too vulgar—to serve
them in their later business and legal careers, their preferred
professional destinations. They also served another purpose,
which a less fastidious age might have described as a marriage
market.

Scholarly distinction, in the more precise meaning of that
term, counted for relatively little in this society. Though a
school like Phillips Andover boasted an excellent faculty, concerned to instruct in morals as well as math, believing that
Latin and Greek ought not to be viewed as exotic languages,
intellectual accomplishment per se was not the measure of
success for either the boys or their teachers. For all his obvious
academic limitations, Andover gave George Bush precisely the
passport he required to move on to his next intended desti-
nation, Yale. Adolf Hitler, however, caused those plans to be
delayed, at least for a time. The country was at war, and Bush,
like others of his social class, enlisted. Again convention required that he serve as an officer. Joining the Navy, he trained
as a pilot, and ended his career as a lieutenant junior grade.
Had he chosen a branch of the service where the training was
less arduous and less technical, he might have risen higher.
The recipient of a Distinguished Flying Cross, as well as other
decorations, he proved himself faithful to traditions his father's
generation extolled and propagated.

At Yale, a married undergraduate, he lived a life different
from that he would have known had the war not intervened.
His marriage to Barbara Pierce early in 1945 made him anxious

to conclude his studies and get on with the real business of living. Never a scholar, he prized particularly his Skull and Bones membership, a social distinction whose value both he and his father appreciated. It brought him in touch again with his own, those he expected to spend the rest of his life with. Whether or not his father's entry into the Senate, following on his graduation from Yale, gave him the first hint of a possible future career, it is significant that he chose not to pursue further studies in law school or business school—two of the preferred next stops for others who shared his privileged life experience—but that he chose to move to Texas, hoping to add to his fortune there, gaining a new kind of financial independence.

His Texas years remain the least known. In Bush mythology, they represent the time when he made it on his own. No son of a United States senator, with a Yale degree, a Skull and Bones connection, a record of decorated war service, and a talent for sports was starting out as the boy no one knew, who would make it wholly on his own in that new and dangerous frontier called oil-rich Texas. The fact that he was co-founder and director of the Zapata Petroleum Corporation before he was thirty suggests that some of his own or his father's money helped create a niche for him; that he became president of the Zapata Off Shore Company in 1956 and chairman of the board in 1964 suggests business success.

Like so many others in the 1950s and 1960s—including some who started out with fewer social advantages—Bush accumulated a fairly substantial fortune. One of the more remarkable features of the postwar world, and not only in the United States, was the ease with which many made money rapidly, joining an ever-expanding company of the very rich. The Cold War, in creating large federally guaranteed markets for many commodities—and not only those required in the purely military sector—gave an impetus to industrial expansion. The baby boom created new cities and suburban towns and generated a demand for consumer goods of every variety. The postwar prosperity, particularly in its early period, took a form very different from that of the 1920s; it drew its distinctive features from satisfying substantial deferred consumer demands, but also from serving an insatiable federal appetite for Cold War defenses and real war expenditures, first in Korea, then in Vietnam. George Bush, like so many others of his generation, rose with the economic tide; his fortune made, he prepared to go home again, to the East, retaining his Texas "roots." He chose Washington, D.C., a city he knew.

How did his Texas years change him? Had good fortune made him more worldly? Did the hardness and toughness of Houston give him the grit that others of his generation acquired through adversity? Bush had been fortunate in all things: parents, wife, education, business. Still, these did not give him conspicuous or immediate success in politics. Contesting a seat for the United States Senate in 1964, he failed to win it. Twice elected representative for the 7th Texas District, he served in both the 90th and the 91st Congress, but saw at once that this was not the life he aspired to. Impatient with a career that did not fulfill his earlier Andover, Navy, Yale, and Texas promise, he sought something that would carry more substantial power and prestige. Bush arrived in Washington a wealthy man, well connected; the Old Blue Mafia boasted influence in the capital, awarding Skull and Bones the weight appropriate to a secret society known to be fastidious in estimating an individual's success potential. Bush searched for an early release from a dead-end post, which made him subservient to demanding Texas constituents. It took no great insight for him to see that his emancipation from the House depended on Richard Nixon's winning the 1968 elections. When that happened, to Bush's intense satisfaction, he was on his way up. In theory, this was the start of George Bush's political ascent; in fact, it was less important than the events that would occur eight years later when Gerald Ford lost to Jimmy Carter.

The great positions that Bush listed on his résumé after
1971—United States Ambassador to the United Nations, Director of the Central Intelligence Agency, chief of the United
States Liaison Office in the People's Republic of China, and
chairman of the Republican National Committee—counted for
very little in persuading others that he was presidential timber.
What mattered, and was too rarely remarked on, was President
Carter's political example, which gave Bush the idea that he,
too, could become President, not in some distant future, but
in 1980. Carter, by his obscurity, having never served in any
official capacity more important than that of governor of
Georgia, and then for only a brief time, provided the example
that Bush, assisted by his Texas friend James Baker, ingeniously
used in putting himself forward for his own party's nomination
for the presidency. It was a bold stroke, without hazard,
reasonable in a campaign where his chief competitor was likely
to be an old man, a former movie star who had recently served
as governor of California. While Bush failed in his prime
objective, his battle allowed him to win second prize, a substantial one: the vice presidency.

He entered the service of Ronald Reagan, the man who beat
him, who had been told that the loyal Republican from Texas
would add considerable weight to the Republican Party ticket.
The whole thing was arranged by Baker, who did for Bush
what Robert Kennedy once did for his brother: he managed
his campaign in a more fundamental sense than is suggested
by those lame and inadequate words. With Baker as his
counselor, Bush acquired a precious human resource: Baker
knew how to manufacture a presidential candidacy. He had
learned a great deal from watching Jimmy Carter win, and he
hoped to use that knowledge to elevate George Bush to some
place on the party ticket.

Independently wealthy, Bush was in a position to spend four
years winning the presidential nomination; no compelling
financial needs required him to work; having no profession

other than that of politician, the fig leaf common to others with his aspirations—lawyers like Richard Nixon, for example—was not immediately available to him. Such men, Republicans and Democrats, characteristically took temporary refuge in a law partnership where they actively, and not always very secretly, pursued their political ambitions. Bush lacked such an obvious professional cover. Still, because it was convenient (and important) to have an office to go to, a legitimate business address and connection that would appear to be fully occupying him, Bush became a member of the executive committee of the First International Bank of Houston. It was a perfect sinecure; it allowed his presidential campaign to go forward, and it gave him the full-time services of his rich and talented Texas friend Baker, who was ready to guide him in his search for the all-important political presidential fuel, campaign monies.

Bush was certainly not Nelson Rockefeller, neither in the size of his pocketbook nor in his willingness to dip into it, not even for a coveted White House tenancy. As he crisscrossed the country, calling on many he had first come to know as chairman of the Republican National Committee, he realized how hard the fight to win the party's nomination would be. The former governor of California, Ronald Reagan, amply financed, with a splendid reputation for what he had done as governor, stood in his way. Still, through a close study of the 1976 campaign—Ford's failure and Carter's success—Bush came away believing that it could be done. Literally taking whole pages out of the Carter success book, he recognized the supreme importance of the Iowa primary. It was in Iowa that Carter, in his remarkable upset victory, had taken the first major steps on his journey to the White House. A comparable strategy might conceivably work a second time, for another unknown.

In May 1979, Bush announced his candidacy, and in the weeks before the Iowa primary in January 1980 spent an extraordinary amount of time seeking to make himself known. His chief rival, Ronald Reagan, neither as industrious nor as importunate, felt no comparable need to make Iowa his temporary home. When the caucus results were tallied, Bush was found to have beaten Reagan, narrowly, 31 to 29 percent. While the margin of the victory was small, its publicity value, particularly with the media, was immense. Bush had suddenly emerged from a Republican pack with many runners, including men as conspicuous as Senator Howard Baker and as inconspicuous as Representative John Anderson, to appear to be a powerful contender. The next hurdle would be the New Hampshire primary. While the influential publisher of the Manchester *Union-Leader*, William Loeb, thought Bush a liberal lightweight, his opposition only helped Bush; if Loeb found it necessary to be so violent in his attacks, it could only be because Bush represented a real threat to the conservative favorite, Ronald Reagan.

Some of this unquestioned advantage, which might have done something to give Bush liberal Republican and independent support—the breed existed in New Hampshire—was thrown away by Bush when, in a debate organized by the Nashua *Telegraph*, billed as a one-to-one confrontation between Reagan and Bush, Howard Baker and John Anderson appeared, demanding that they, too, be allowed to participate. Reagan, in his usual self-confident way, was willing for them to join in the free-for-all. Bush, in a rare display of public temper, insisted on keeping to the letter of the agreement his managers had made with the Reagan staff. He would not allow it. In the end, Bush lost, on both counts; the debate proceeded with all four mouthing their platitudes, and Bush came across as a spoilsport. The incident, insignificant in itself, probably had little effect on the final New Hampshire primary results, but it suggested something of the personalities of the two men. Bush lost and Reagan won, in the balloting as on the television screen.

In the next major primary, in Massachusetts, Bush barely defeated the Republican "dark horse" candidate, John Anderson; he won much more convincingly in Connecticut, one of his several "home" states. The Florida results were a disaster; Reagan won with an overwhelming vote of 57 percent, Bush managing to register only 30 percent. In Pennsylvania, a key state, as significant as Florida, Bush raised himself from the floor; he carried the state against Reagan, with a respectable 53 to 46 percent showing; he then went on to victory in Michigan. Clearly, he enjoyed support in several parts of the country, but the two decisive primaries, in California and Ohio, lay ahead, and the universal media opinion, based on extensive polling, indicated that Reagan would win both. For many Americans who received all their news from television, the battle was over. Reagan would be the Republican Party's standard bearer; there was no way to stop him.

During the Memorial Day weekend, Bush concluded that the public opinion polls were accurate; there was little point in continuing the struggle. Lacking the funds needed for the large June primaries, but more importantly, being unwilling to see himself go down to all but certain defeat, he decided the time had come to end his campaign. Informing Reagan of his decision, he added, significantly, that if anyone approached the former California governor wishing to promote his candidacy for the vice presidency, Reagan was to understand that this was being done without his consent. Bush avoided any suggestion that he would refuse a Reagan invitation to join him on the Republican Party ticket; he simply wanted the governor to know that he was not pushing himself. The Connecticut Yankee, Texas millionaire, Maine summer resident, and denizen of Washington, D.C., who had relied on others for all his appointive offices, was not to be thought of as promoting himself.

At the Republican Party convention, in Detroit, the Reagan nomination was assured. The only question: who would be his nominee for Vice President? Given what many recognized to be certain of Reagan's more obvious lacks, some, including Henry Kissinger, imagined that Gerald Ford might be a reasonable choice. Given Ford's experience as President in the difficult years following Watergate, he was represented as someone who could greatly assist the next President, complementing him in any number of ways. Indeed, the idea of a "co-presidency" was bruited, though political wisdom recommended that no such outlandish and novel proposal be formally advanced. Still, a Ford candidacy offered many advantages; he would provide geographic balance; he knew Congress intimately, having served for decades in the House of Representatives; he had experience in the White House. It was not to be. George Bush, the man who secured the second-largest number of votes in the Republican primaries, was chosen. James Baker did a great deal to guarantee that his man, the man of the future, and not Henry Kissinger's, the defeated candidate of 1976, received Ronald Reagan's nod.

Given Reagan's reputation for being a Goldwater Republican, the choice of Bush was thought to be the selection of a moderate, a Republican of the center. *The New York Times*, in its post-convention editorial, thought Bush a "serious, able and likable man." If the accolade seemed somewhat tepid, the additional protest that "Ronald Reagan's second choice is not second-rate" seemed positively insulting. Who had ever suggested that Bush was "second-rate"? In fact, *The Washington Post* came very close to saying precisely that; its editorial, more critical of the nominee, and more biting, included the words: "Anyone who thinks that George Bush is a liberal is not one himself. . . . George Bush does not exactly pose a huge danger to the republic from the left. He is rather a center-right traditionalist, establishment-oriented competent government figure who showed himself to be resilient but not especially presidential in the campaign."

Bush had not secured what he most wished to have, but

something almost as good. The President was old, and there was always the possibility of his falling seriously ill or dying during his term. What no one could have prophesied was a would-be assassin's attack that almost took the President's life within three months of his coming into office. For hours, certainly, for those who knew the situation best, an early Bush presidency was not ruled out. Still, the succession did not come quite so quickly or so easily. Bush had to live through eight long years as Vice President, comporting himself much as Richard Nixon did in the same office more than two decades earlier.

In 1988, Bush, Reagan's creation, had his reward; he won the nomination easily. He went on to win the election, just as easily, but not with quite the same studied elegance or innocent insouciance that Reagan habitually managed. Flaying at his rival, the unfortunate Michael Dukakis, the Connecticut Yankee showed his true colors; he was not a Republican in the Massachusetts tradition; neither a Leverett Saltonstall nor a Cabot Lodge, he showed himself mean in the way Lyndon Johnson could be, in the way that many other Texans, sometimes unfairly, were said to be. The question, wholly unanswerable, was whether Bush's hard-bitten Yankee nature showed in his encounter with the diminutive son of Greek immigrants, whom he despised only slightly less than Jimmy Carter, or whether his behavior simply reflected the hazards of having spent so much of his adult life in dubious company.

The campaign would be remembered, and not only by Democrats, for Willie Horton, a black first-degree murderer, given a weekend furlough from his prison in accordance with penal regulations that existed in Massachusetts, who then committed a stabbing and a rape. It was this kind of "permissiveness" that the nation needed to be protected against. In the television commercial that featured the incident, the implied racism was offered in a code which every white (and black) citizen would certainly understand. It was more than just an attack on a too liberal governor of a too liberal state, and more than the dirty trick of a subordinate, a tough who would repent of his excesses before his premature death a few years later. In this, as in so many other of the so-called political issues, including that of respect for the "flag," the Vice President showed a cheapness that reflected something other than the excitement incidental to a presidential campaign. The Vice President was well aware of what he did during the campaign to blacken the reputation of someone who had some experience of foul play on Beacon Hill but had no notion of the dimensions it could take in Washington. The White House prize was thought sufficient to excuse every act, every word.

The Bush inaugural address suggested something of the poverty of his conception of the office he had been called to. Indeed, it was largely an inspirational message, wholly lacking in specific content and filled with the kind of religious symbolism that Ronald Reagan habitually used. Foreign policy figured scarcely at all; Bush had learned too much during his years of Reagan service to imagine that this was a subject the nation cared deeply about. Knowing that the television audience waited to be inspired, he was more than ready to carry on in the tradition of the former President who sat just a few feet from him; he gave what he imagined the occasion called for. The speech, written by Peggy Noonan, who had recently crafted Ronald Reagan's farewell address, reeked of sentimentality; it resembled no other in the long history of the republic. Delivered from "democracy's front porch," the nation's Bicentennial Inaugural, the speech was maudlin when it was not positively embarrassing. The President saw the totalitarian era as passing, "its old ideas blown away like leaves from an ancient, lifeless tree." "Free markets, free speech, free elections and the exercise of free will unhampered by the state" was the world's assured destiny.

Reverting always to his religious imagery and theme, the President said: "I take as my guide the hope of a saint: In crucial things, unity—in important things, diversity—in all things, generosity." The country, "proud, free, decent, and civil," knew that material goods were of small account. Children needed to be taught "what it means to be a loyal friend, a loving parent, a citizen who leaves his home, his neighborhood and town better than he found it." To help with making "better hearts and finer souls" was a worthy presidential objective, though admittedly difficult to achieve. America was never great except when committed to high moral principle—"to make kinder the face of the nation and gentler the face of the world." Homelessness, drug addiction, crime—these were all modern scourges. The President, disciple of a worthy teacher, said, "The old solution, the old way, was to think that public money alone could end these problems. But we have learned that is not so. And in any case, our funds are low: We have a deficit to bring down. We have more will than wallet: but will is what we need."

The "goodness and the courage of the American people" were the only resources that grew in time of need. The President relied on both. He spoke of a new activism, "harnessing the unused talent of the elderly and the unfocused energy of the young," working together in a "thousand points of light," the community organizations of the country. "Duty, sacrifice, commitment, and a patriotism that finds its expression in taking part and pitching in," was what America was all about. The nation could not continue to be sundered by the memories of Vietnam. Compromise and harmony were to be the new watchwords. The Congress and the executive needed again to work together.

The man who had so emphasized his experience—so different from that of his provincial rival, the governor of Massachusetts—addressed few remarks to or about the world outside. Those he used were vague, illustrative of an American foreign policy that had itself become barren of ideas and principles. The United States would remain strong to keep the peace; it would be true to its word. The President intoned: "Great nations like great men must keep their word." Alliances would be maintained, the American "closeness" with the Soviet Union retained, "consistent with our security and with progress," a phrase of something less than absolute clarity. In acknowledging that he was "neither prince nor Pope," he sought not "a window on men's souls" but greater tolerance. These were the President's words of hope and promise, as given on January 20, 1989.

In the months that followed, it was impossible not to believe that the President was endowed with the kind of good fortune that made it reasonable for anyone, including his friends, to dub him "lucky George." The "evil empire," once proclaimed so dangerous, seemed to be in an advanced state of disintegration. The Soviet Union, contrary to what certain of Reagan's disciples said, was not pushed into bankruptcy by being required to compete militarily with the United States; the Eastern European "people's democracies" were not finally rising because the United States, over many decades, had recommended they do so. The events in the Soviet Union and Central and Eastern Europe owed more to conditions internal to the Communist world—political, moral, and economic—than to any created by a far-seeing Republican administration prepared to fight for larger defense expenditures.

Still, 1989 was an *annus mirabilis*, beginning with the wholly peaceful "revolution" in Hungary and ending with the bloodbath in Romania. The President congratulated the world on its good fortune, but had no idea of how to help the newly liberated countries or how to react to growing evidence of public disorder and economic decay in the Soviet Union. Gorbachev showed himself a remarkable leader, trying one tactic one week, another the next, and appealing always to admirers in the West. As helpless before the flood engulfing Eastern and Central Europe as those swept from power, Gorbachev pretended to be in command. President Bush could not even conceive what he himself might do to steer events. In his foreign policy innocence, he saw neither opportunity nor challenge.

He lacked both the words and the policies to encourage those in Eastern Europe who had recently broken out of what they regarded as their Communist prisons. In July, in Warsaw, the President performed miserably. Given the admiration and sympathy Poland expressed for the United States during the whole period of Communist domination, despite unconcealed dismay with Roosevelt's Yalta accords, the President was provided an opportunity to make a memorable statement. He had no wish to do so; Polish expectations of United States aid ought not to be encouraged. In the circumstances, he delivered a speech of astonishing banality. The gesture was calculated. In his mind, the United States was poor; the Poles ought not to live with the illusion that Uncle Sam would soon be arriving with a bag full of "goodies." Having no money to give, he lacked the will, but also the imagination and knowledge to propose other benefits, working in collaboration with the European Community, to devise policies to help a friendly country devastated by war and four decades of Soviet exploitation.

Bush had no sense of how World War II had decimated Poland; he scarcely appreciated why Bonn, for all its pretended concern with Poland's welfare, could never be wholly forgiven for what Germans, in another time, had done. Nor could he begin to understand the ways in which Catholic Poland detested an atheist society across its borders, not only for the Katyn massacre, the Soviet-German pact, and the hundreds of thousands who suffered at Stalin's hands, but also for its exploitation over decades of a people quite literally helpless before its military power. The failure to promise more in specific monetary engagements, given the U.S. federal budget situation, was understandable. The failure even to conceptualize what the American colossus might wish to do showed characteristic shortsightedness, a lack of empathy that seemed almost insulting. Poland, for the President, was one stop on a very crowded European itinerary.

In Hungary, where he spent a little over twenty-four hours, he delivered a speech of unusual obtuseness, scarcely attenuated by its pretended philanthropy. The President, to a sympathetic auditor, appeared to be going through the motions required of an American President on a state visit. He had no time for Budapest because he could not imagine using its peaceful revolution for larger purposes. His ignorance of history showed; so, also, did his decades-long imprisonment in Cold War Republican administrations. As in Poland, neither the President nor his Secretary of State could place the Hungarian situation in a larger European or world context.

In all this, the President remained his usual distant self, cool, calm, uninvolved, courteous, correct. His failure to perceive how the United States might relate to what was unfolding, already evident in the first days of July, showed itself repeatedly and more emphatically in the months that followed, when even more dramatic happenings captured the attention of Europe, and became the daily fare of ardent and committed American television news watchers. With access to information not vouchsafed to ordinary citizens, the President sat back and watched, pretending to understand what had become a momentous year in European history.

Events in the Soviet Union, particularly in the Baltic republics, might have been thought legitimately preoccupying. There, tensions were rising. The Soviet leadership, having acknowledged early in August that there had been secret protocols to the 1939 Nazi-Soviet nonaggression pact—a fact long known outside the Soviet Union—and that these had mandated the partition of Poland, giving a "free hand" to the Soviet Union in Estonia, Latvia, and Lithuania, set the stage for mass demonstrations in all three republics, coinciding with the fiftieth anniversary of the pact's signature. A human chain, linking more than a million men and women, stretched from Tallinn in Estonia through Riga in Latvia to Vilnius in Lithuania, all in protest of an unjust Soviet occupation that made them unwilling subjects of the Kremlin. Though the United States had never officially recognized the incorporation of the three Baltic states into the Soviet Union, this symbolic and vivid demonstration of their will to break away was not one the President chose to comment on.

When, on September 9, Boris Yeltsin arrived in New York for an eight-day American speaking tour, it was not at all certain that the White House would even receive him. No one had any interest in offending Mikhail Gorbachev; in any case, there was no wish to send the wrong message to the Russian people. The Bush administration, like the one that preceded it, was perpetually preoccupied with the messages being sent into the world. It took for granted that the whole world was watching the White House, the political center of the universe. In the end, the President's National Security Adviser, Brent Scowcroft, agreed to see Yeltsin, and the President spent a few minutes with him. Few in the country at the time knew who Yeltsin was or what he represented. When, however, the Italian newspaper *La Repubblica* printed articles suggesting that Yeltsin was a heavy drinker who spent great amounts of money in an American shopping spree, *Pravda* reprinted the story, and American newspapers had the "scoop" they were looking for. It was all a good late summer's entertainment. This was a news item calculated to capture the American public's fancy, filled as it was with "human interest."

On October 23, the Soviet Foreign Minister, speaking before the Supreme Soviet, said that the Soviet intervention in Afghanistan "violated the norms of proper behavior . . . [and] general human values," conceding also that the building of the radar at Krasnoyarsk violated the 1972 ABM treaty. It appeared more obvious than ever that the United States and the Soviet Union understood each other, that the two had come together in a quite remarkable way. Indeed, in both countries, it seemed as if Soviet-American understanding was in some mysterious way fueling the Eastern European "revolution," if so grandiose a term could be applied to disparate events whose pattern remained unclear. In fact, much of what was happening in Eastern Europe depended not at all on the United States, and only incidentally on decisions taken in the Soviet Union. Still, Gorbachev's insistence that he had "absolute respect" for the integrity of all states, that the Soviet Union had no interest in interfering in the affairs of others, constantly repeated, was having an effect, though by itself it did not account for the October events in the German Democratic Republic.

Throughout Communist Europe, history was being rewritten. In East Germany, Czechoslovakia, Lithuania, and Romania, the upheavals continued. Following on the revolutionary changes already registered in Poland and Hungary, the whole of Central and Eastern Europe seemed in ferment. In the United States, all the old standard scripts were still used. Nothing was thought to excite public interest more than a meeting of the two most powerful men in the world, the leaders of the United States and the Soviet Union. If Europe was transfixed by its revolutions, the United States was preoccupied with the Malta summit. Gorbachev, on his way to Malta, stopped in Rome, where he spoke again of the "Common European Home," in his imagination a commonwealth of sovereign and economically interdependent peoples. In Malta, Bush presented the American proposals: a bilateral agreement banning shipboard tactical nuclear weapons; a strategic arms control treaty to be signed by June 1990; a treaty on mutual reduction of conventional forces, to be signed by the end of 1990; an end to U.S. chemical weapons production as soon as all nations capable of producing such weapons had signed an international convention outlawing them; liberalization of U.S.-Soviet trade, contingent on the easing of Soviet emigration policies. The Soviets were asked to halt their supply of weapons to the leftist rebels in El Salvador.

The conference was noteworthy mostly for the weather. Those who planned it knew nothing of early Mediterranean winters. At the press conference, which followed on December 3, each leader expressed pleasure with the summit results, but Gorbachev denied the American charge that the Soviet Union was continuing to arm the Salvadoran rebels. The Malta summit was a memorable media event; the ships bobbing in the stormy seas gave photographers an incomparable opportunity to record a scene that made the encounter different from any Reagan and Gorbachev had staged. The vast company of reporters, assembled to cover a historic event, had very little to report, but this did not prevent them from babbling on hour after hour. The American-Soviet friendship continued, and this was thought news enough for a world far more intrigued by the remarkable events in Eastern Europe.

What a year! What an inheritance, even if unearned, for a new American President! How did he see it all, as 1990 approached? What advantages could he perceive from what had happened to weaken and sometimes destroy Communist authority in Europe? The President's statements were measured and few; his pleasure was obvious, but his plans were obscure. In a fundamental sense, 1989 brought the President a harvest he could not himself have hoped for, or indeed planted. Did Bush have any premonition that the Gorbachev political "honeymoon," still very alive in foreign parts, had ended in the Soviet Union and that this constituted a threat to his continued rule? As the United States settled down to what it expected to be an even better year, almost no one asked whether the transition to democracy in Central Europe would be hard or easy, whether Communism was as wounded as it appeared to be, whether the President, constantly repeating that the Cold War was over, understood the implications of his own remarks.

If the Cold War was indeed over, then American foreign policy had to be dramatically altered. The President's political life had been in the service of men who made the Soviet Union their chief concern. What ought the new American foreign policy interest be? Where would the President receive his instruction? Not from the Secretary of State, who knew even less than he did, and not from his National Security Adviser, who was expert mostly in Cold War diplomacy. It became necessary to think of what other intellectual and political resources the President commanded. The omens were not wholly favorable. Reputed neither for his wide reading nor for his deep thinking, the President was not a man accustomed to change.

Would the President's ignorance of foreign policy lead him astray, even in his relations with the Soviet Union, let alone with Europe, the Middle East, and the so-called Third World? Without being a disciple of either Henry Kissinger or Jeane Kirkpatrick, did he understand the nature of authoritarian governments? If he did not, how could he hope to deal with Saudi Arabia, Kuwait, or Iraq, not to speak of the Soviet Union, China, and Cuba? In his elaborate defense of free markets, did he understand the reasons for the inefficiency of Communist economies, and not only in the Soviet Union? Had he himself been taken in by the myths that had been perpetrated for so long on why Germans, even under Communism, prospered? And how could he hope to understand modern Japan if he imagined always that it was a brilliant American occupation policy that had created its postwar prosperity? Did he realize the extent of America's own social devastation? Did he understand how perceived economic weakness would limit and shape any foreign policy initiatives that others might wish to press on him?

Given the President's vague and rhetorical explanations of what 1989 had been, of what 1990 might be, there was reason to believe that he understood little of the dynamics of late-twentieth-century revolution. If he failed to understand the reasons for the collapse of Communism—a system based on hierarchy that concealed its true character, pretending to be egalitarian when it was in fact privileged, legitimating its extraordinary actions by reference always to a foreign enemy —it was because he too lived in a closed world, the prisoner of a mind-set that had its origins in the Cold War.

While Gorbachev, knowing Soviet weaknesses, sought desperately to deal with some, concealing only their complexity and difficulty because he hoped somehow to be able to maintain the Communist Party in power, Bush had yet to acknowledge the American dilemma. Like his predecessor, he refused to cope with the explosive issue of race; like others of his social class and generation, he was puzzled by America's economic sclerosis, which he confidently expected would be relieved with the ending of what was euphemistically described as a recession. Believing in the political system that made the Republican Party the White House party, as it had been for almost half a century after the beginning of the Civil War, he never once reflected on what Cold War politics had done to weaken what had once passed for a polity of discussion, where power was shared with Congress.

Bush never imagined that there was a desperate need to reconsider American foreign policy; he would not have known how to begin to do that, failing to understand the inextricable connections between domestic and foreign policy. He lived in a Nixon-Reagan era when these were largely separable entities, managed separately. If vigilance against foreign enemies had made the country triumphant, at least in its own vivid imagination, what would serve as the new national goad? What, indeed, would the new foreign policy problems be when they did not relate principally to the dangers of Soviet aggression, when they did not involve the perpetual search for containing the new latter-day Hitlers?

The President assumed that all would go on as it had throughout his political lifetime. His lack of knowledge and imagination reflected an incapacity to take in the meaning of world events shaped by many contradictory forces: revolutionary technology and new modes of communication, ideologies that emphasized human rights and human dignity and others that looked for both in the revival of traditional religions, sacred and secular. In his simple explanations of why Communism had failed, he saw mostly the failure of a command economy; free markets would resolve the problems of peoples too long kept in Communist thrall. No one told the President that these same remedies had been proposed after World War I, to recapture the happy world that had existed before 1914. No one thought to explain what the 1920s had been, not in Calvin Coolidge's America, but in that more complex world of those who had suffered the war, whose lives had been transformed by it, as so many others had been by decades of the Cold War. The President and his chief Cabinet colleagues were provincials, made so not so much by their origins as by an education too limited, a life experience, particularly in or near the White House, that made them incapable of understanding larger world currents. Consumed with winning elections, uninterested in the complex and varied world that lay outside America's frontiers, they showed the characteristic faults of men unmindful of change, ignorant of history.

If the President's sentiments of pleasure and relief with the events unfolding in the Communist world were mixed at all with a sense of foreboding, he concealed his misgivings. A younger man than his predecessor, he was equally inclined to sit and wait, hoping for something to happen. When it did, as in Eastern Europe, he continued to sit. How to use the revolutionary events occurring there to realize larger American objectives, how to make democracy a more potent force in the world, how to harness foreign policy bonuses to spur genuine domestic economic and social reform—these did not seem even to occur to him or to his Secretary of State as reasonable policy goals.

Neither understood the fragility of Gorbachev's situation in the Soviet Union; neither was willing to acknowledge that he might not be around forever. If the Cold War was indeed over, at least in one of its guises, accommodating leaders in the Kremlin might not survive for very long; a new kind of dictatorship, less dominated by a Marxist veneer, might soon emerge, with or without Gorbachev at its head, presiding over a nation more xenophobic than any that had existed since 1917. The President saw no necessity to treat with the "opposition" in the Soviet Union; he scarcely knew it, and had he informed himself of its character, he would have been shocked by its principles. In any case, to do so would have been, in his mind, to betray a power that existed, preferring a power that might never be.

He was equally inept in treating with the Chinese who rebelled in Tiananmen Square, preferring to deal with those who gave the military their orders to shoot. Those sympathetic to what they saw as the prudent course he adopted constantly referred back to the dark age when the United States, unwisely, sought to "quarantine" an aggressive and authoritarian Communist China. Wisdom lay in negotiating with the powers that existed. No President, in the view of those who accepted this stance, could afford to thwart the leaders of a powerful and independent China, a nation of a billion people. The President watched, as did more ordinary citizens, on television, of course, the murder of young Chinese students. Some claimed that as many as 5,000 men and women died in the Beijing massacre; other thousands were reportedly injured. The arrests of yet additional thousands did not play on American television, and therefore entered America's consciousness less. In this, as in everything, the President had a number of options. He chose the easiest—to do nothing.

His limited experience in life could in some measure explain his wish to hold high office without having any sense of how to use that office to serve the commonweal. Others, less charitably, might argue that his social conscience had been atrophied by too long service in Ronald Reagan's court. A more convincing explanation would be that, like many Americans of his generation, Bush had become so habituated to living with the Cold War, was so much formed by its values, that he lacked any moral or political compass to guide him when he wished to turn away from its simple and brutal verities. If Soviet politicians and bureaucrats found a political U-turn a difficult one to negotiate, why should Americans, whose careers were constructed on an analogous experience, be more adept in doing so? No one asked that question; it was a painfully embarrassing one.

Yet it struck at the heart of a situation too few in the United States reflected on. World War II was the last universal triumph that all Americans—Republicans and Democrats—were able to exult in. World War II was the nation's glorious apotheosis, even if Roosevelt, anathema to many right-wing Republicans, was its putative manager. Americans lived with the illusion that war provided solutions. War certainly annihilated Nazism; the American victory converted aggressive imperial Japan into a pacific society. War, in the decades that followed, took on a less attractive patina, and not only because of Vietnam. Because of the awesome power of thermonuclear weapons, war was never a very live option in the one international rivalry that mattered, with the Soviet Union. There, peaceful coexistence, based on redundant armament, was the answer; elsewhere, particularly with small and, by definition, inferior states, war might still be conceived, at least by the United States. The President found it easy to attack Panama—in a just cause, of course—as his predecessor had attacked, with even greater impunity, mighty Libya and tiny Grenada.

Bush lived with these memories, but also with these models. He lived with yet another, which he owed as much to the despised Democrats as to his fellow Republicans. War, a solution for certain international difficulties, was an incomparable rhetorical remedy also for internal disasters. So, after George Bush came to the White House, in his insipid and lackluster inaugural address, he pledged a new war, a "War against

Drugs." Poverty, too large and complex, gave way to a more manageable internal foe, a threat to the nation's youth, to its future. To give directions in the field, he chose William Bennett, who took "lip" from no one, least of all namby-pamby Democrats. The tactics would be dramatic; again, in the absence of money—a deficit-laden federal government could not be expected to contribute very much—the threat of long prison terms, more efficient police surveillance, and action against suspected and known dealers were thought to offer promise. So, also, in time, efforts would be made to educate the users, employing all the powers of exhortation to reach and reform them. Finally, pressure would be applied to deter rogue nations, mostly in Latin America, from entrapping hundreds of thousands of innocent young Americans, insufficiently informed about the devil they were being invited to sup with. The President emphasized the power of persuasion; education about drugs would do much to remedy the situation.

The low-cost operation was launched, and soon Bennett claimed his victories, which existed more in his imagination than in the streets of the capital, not to speak of those of New York, Detroit, Cleveland, Los Angeles, and any number of other drug-beleaguered American cities. When, after almost two years, Bennett realized that the "war" was without either strategy or victory, he, like so many others, decided that he could no longer sacrifice himself on the altar of a federal salary. The field commander left, and the program, such as it was, remained. Could even the President imagine that the "war" was going well?

Again, one returns to the question that cries out for an answer. Did the President realize the extent to which he inherited an office, enjoyed it, never intending to grapple with large problems, either in the foreign field or in the domestic? His lame speeches reflected something other than the limited skills of untalented White House speechwriters. Their very imprecision derived from a more serious condition: no more was said because there was nothing more to say. The President, not searching for new ideas or for new proposals to cope with novel opportunities at home or abroad, neither perceived them nor imagined there was an imperative reason to define them. He played the game as Ronald Reagan taught him to play it. Sufficient to the day was the avoidance of all difficulties that might in any way jeopardize his second term, the *summum bonum* of his presidential ambition.

That he lacked any notion of what to do about Eastern Europe was obvious. The vague talk of a Marshall Plan, which came principally from others, scarcely commended itself to someone who knew how limited were the Treasury's assets. The United States of 1989–90 was not the United States of 1947–48; the country lacked the resources and the will to launch venturesome and expensive foreign policy initiatives. In any case, no comparable ideas existed in 1989. Those who advised President Bush, while delighted with the ending of the Cold War, had no notion of what the event portended. To have understood 1989 and appreciated its potential, seeing it as something other than the triumph of an abstract "democracy" and of "free markets," would have required an appreciation of all that had changed in the world since the time of Winston Churchill and Charles de Gaulle, and why rhetoric alone, with its promise of economic abundance, would never suffice to dampen fires ignited by nationalism and race, with deep historic roots, which had only been superficially covered up by Communist repression. George Bush, having received instruction from Ronald Reagan and Richard Nixon, knew how to win elections and swim in Cold War waters. He knew nothing of navigation in a world where the new heads of state were frequently men recently liberated, not only from prisons but from myths, the most confining being that Communism would last forever.

Gorbachev imagined he knew the truth; his years in the KGB told him what others also knew. There was a compelling need for radical economic change. He chose the term *perestroika* to advertise a campaign to achieve dramatic improvements in economic performance, to be accomplished largely through bureaucratic reorganization. In time, the term took on wholly other meanings, used almost indiscriminately to suggest the need for "radical reform," "revolutionary change," "new thinking," and "democratization." Exhortation was expected to create a new spirit in the nation, one which would make Soviet men and women do what they had not done for decades, work. The best-kept secret of Soviet European Communism, that workers received a pittance for their labor and generally reciprocated by doing little, had created a leisured society of bored indolence.

A process that began with Khrushchev, with his revelations about Stalinism, reached a point few had anticipated. A Communist ideology once believed in lost its appeal; a system of Party control and secret-police surveillance, once feared, was reduced to a shambles. The nationalities, represented in Soviet mythology as contented peoples, all equal, began to rebel openly, arguing for liberation from the Soviet yoke. Gorbachev, buffeted on every side, invented yet new slogans; he wished to be known for his efforts to "democratize" the Soviet Union. Greatly admired abroad, the new initiatives produced unintended consequences at home. A genuine left opposition appeared, undisciplined and chaotic, ready to argue that *perestroika* was not working, that far-reaching economic and social reforms were needed. In a matter of months, the Soviet Union began to have something that resembled a "civil society"; men and women, independently organized, began to demand political reform; no Soviet precedent existed for such activity. The country craved an exit from Communism, but there was no easy way out. Did Bush perceive the fragility of the Soviet regime? Was anyone in his circle able to suggest the true extent of Gorbachev's plight?

A gifted man charged with American foreign policy might

have known that this was one of the more likely outcomes of
1989, and might have prepared himself and the country for
the eventuality. The President, incapable of such understanding
or foresight, saw no need for reinsurance. If events in the
Soviet Union became ugly, he would simply return to a version
of older policies. He did nothing in early 1990 to suggest that
he recognized the precariousness of Gorbachev's position.
Lacking ideas on how to treat the Soviet Union—a country he
reputedly knew a great deal about from his UN and CIA
experiences—he was even more inept when it came to devising
policies for the former Communist states of Eastern and Central
Europe. Again, how could it have been otherwise? These states
had never been central concerns of the President, having
figured little in the foreign policy discussions of the Reagan
years; collectively, they represented little in his calculus of state
power.

When, therefore, he was required to deal with a man like
Václav Havel, the newly elected President of a democratic
Czechoslovakia, his difficulties derived not from his being
uncomfortable in the presence of an intellectual, a playwright
to boot, and a very recent convert to politics, but from something infinitely more important. The President's experience
had been with men accustomed to holding power in the
Communist world. He had no notion of how to deal with those
who had suffered from that power. These were not old-time
dissidents, brought in for a single courtesy call, providing the
photo opportunity calculated to win favor with numbers of
Republican right-wing supporters. Something more momentous had happened; the former dissidents were in power;
President Bush scarcely knew how to address them, let alone
how to negotiate with them.

The Soviet leader, Mikhail Gorbachev, awarded the Man of
the Decade title by *Time* magazine, was an individual the
President could deal with. His was an achievement the President
could appreciate. As for Havel, the President neither read his

plays nor knew his tragic tale, except as the media, in their simple distortions, represented both. To see such men only as victims, imprisoned for speaking out, was to convert their epic heroism into prosaic political action. In the case of Havel, he came to the United States to bear witness, to instruct an uninformed President and a cheering Congress in what decades of totalitarian rule had done to once proud societies. He knew what could be said, what could only be faintly hinted at. He came to Congress to attest to a life of suffering, not only or principally his own. Yet he came not in the spirit of revenge but in one of forgiveness, knowing that no other attitude made political or moral sense. If the President was incapable of giving Havel's text a close reading or imagined such a reading to be necessary, there was no one in the White House to interpret it for him. Havel's visit was perceived as an event of less than transcendental importance. So it was with all the other "beggars" from Europe.

In his moving address to Congress, Havel mentioned the Soviet President only twice, at a time when Gorbachev was much esteemed in the United States. Havel spoke of totalitarianism, the only system Eastern Europeans of his generation knew. His message had to do with his own country but also with the Soviet Union. His words were unambiguous; he said: "The Communist type of totalitarian system has left both our nations, Czechs and Slovaks, as it has all the nations of the Soviet Union and the other countries the Soviet Union subjugated in its time, a legacy of countless dead, an infinite spectrum of human suffering, profound economic decline and, above all, enormous human humiliation. It has brought us horrors that fortunately you have not known." It is difficult to know whether those who heard Havel in Washington understood the full significance of his reference to "all the nations of the Soviet Union." Unlike the leaders of Western Europe and the United States, who craved a restoration of order and tranquillity, fearing that dissenters might press their demands too far and insist on independence, the Czech President knew that such demands could not be set aside. For him, nations existed; they had to be accommodated. Any system that sought arbitrarily to maintain a political union that did not represent the will of the peoples expressed through their several cultures was, for him, at risk.

The Czech President, given to understatement, emphasized one of several unstable elements in the Soviet Union which no one could safely ignore. Gorbachev hoped to avoid having to deal with these problems, waiting for a more propitious time. The Czech leader understood that it was impossible for him to do so. Still, he indicated why the Soviet Union merited American sympathy, but only if its objective was the creation of a genuinely pluralist society. While he joined President Bush in recommending a reduction of military forces in Europe, praising both the American and the Soviet leaders for their efforts, recognizing how much arms control contributed to a reduction of international tensions, these were secondary matters for him. The important thing was to maintain the momentum in the Soviet Union and Eastern Europe toward democratic reform.

The distance between what Havel recommended and what President Bush proposed to do was enormous. The world had changed out of all recognition in 1989, and the American President, reputed to possess foreign policy expertise, could not conceive of what to do to take advantage of these changes. His preference was for conventional bilateral arms control negotiations, conducted by experts, which would be periodically blessed in a well-staged and highly advertised summit performance. In his habitual and traditional pose, he sat, waiting for something to happen.

Like his predecessor, the President was prone to take what might most charitably be described as accident-proof police actions. Such operations, fail-safe in every sense of the word, allowed a major power like the United States to publicly castigate and humble a manifestly weaker power, a transgressor in the international arena that could be used as a symbol of how the United States punished an evil it was helpless to deal with at home. Actions of this kind, particularly congenial in circumstances where the hazards of outside interference were nil, gave the appearance of national resolve even when they made no demands of personal sacrifice. What Ronald Reagan had done in Grenada and Libya—not to speak of his equally safe naval actions against Syria—George Bush found it necessary to do in Panama. There, a drug-dealing, American-hating, gun-toting dictator required disciplining. The American military invasion of that Central American republic, a slightly more grandiose and complex replica of Reagan's less remarkable military operation in Grenada—also relatively cost-free, involving few American casualties, the ultimate measure of success—led to a momentary standoff. For a few days at least, the miserable miscreant Panamanian leader, Manuel Noriega, sought and found refuge in Panama City's papal mission. Happily, however, on January 3, 1990, Noriega left that sanctuary and surrendered to the Americans.

With Noriega flown at once by U.S. Drug Enforcement Administration officials to Homestead Air Force Base in Florida, where the long process of bringing him to American justice could begin, the President scored another success. These events, calculated to interest the American media for a full fortnight, had a certain obvious, if only temporary, pictorial appeal. With Noriega safely behind prison bars, the interest in him and in his disordered country, now safely occupied by American troops, fell precipitously. While a few newspapers in the United States (and elsewhere) might complain of how the Americans had comported themselves in this fail-safe operation, such criticism scarcely touched the President. Non-American lives lost—military or civilian—were not thought relevant.

What, in fact, seemed to preoccupy the President? Insofar as foreign policy figured at all, it principally involved two subjects: the unification of the two Germanys and the projected visit of the Soviet President to the United States for a summit conference. Believing that good relations with Germany in the future were all-important, that West Germany was already the most important European Community member, and would become even more so before the end of the century, the President positioned himself to take advantage of that preeminence. It took no courage for him to say that he favored unification; that policy, after all, had been the avowed aim of all his White House predecessors for forty years; to be able to assist in that worthy enterprise was to reinsure himself with the Bonn government, which had already, in any event, secured Soviet consent to unification, taking it out of the President's hands.

When Bush met with Gorbachev in Washington in late May, more than a dozen bilateral accords were signed, dealing with disparate arms control and other related matters. The decisions to reduce strategic nuclear weapons stockpiles, prohibit further production of chemical weapons, and normalize trade relations were significant. Still, such agreements no longer produced the public excitement that had attended American-Soviet negotiations in the Reagan era. What had once seemed extraordinary had become habitual. In these circumstances, the "atmospherics" of the summit, as represented by the media, became all-important. If ships bobbing in the sea was the pictorial image conveyed by Malta, the Gorbachev "walk-about" was *the* event of the Washington summit. To see the Soviet leader moving about as any other biped might in the nation's capital was a photographer's dream, a television spectacular.

A few days after Gorbachev's resounding Washington triumph, another happy event occurred, this time in Copenhagen. The Soviet Foreign Minister surprised his fellow Foreign Ministers at the Conference on Security and Cooperation in Europe (CSCE) with the statement that the Soviet Union was prepared to remove unilaterally all its tactical nuclear weapons stationed in Europe. The Warsaw Pact members, meeting in Moscow a few days later, announced that they no longer viewed the West as an "ideological enemy." The NATO ministers, meeting in Scotland, reciprocated with a declaration complimenting the Warsaw Pact on its "positive spirit." The "era of good feeling" seemed to take on more ample dimensions all the time. These, then, were the principal events that led the leaders of NATO, meeting in London in early July, to issue their "London Declaration," which proposed, quite simply, that the Warsaw Pact and NATO issue a joint statement, declaring the end of their adversarial relationship. President Gorbachev and the other Warsaw Pact leaders, invited to visit NATO headquarters in Brussels, were asked also to "establish regular diplomatic liaison with NATO." The Cold War had passed into history, or so at least it seemed.

During these months of successful European and Soviet negotiations, what had the administration been doing in that other volatile arena, the Middle East? Was the "peace process" being actively pursued? The Secretary of State, as a matter of fact, though increasingly peripatetic, found only limited time to minister to that troubled world. The American mass media, however, claiming to know something of his reputation as a negotiator, appreciating his formidable talents as a lawyer, expected him in time to make a major contribution there. It all depended on the Israelis agreeing to his plans for a peace conference; a change in government, bringing the Labor Party back into office, was expected to help him achieve his aim.

Those who followed Middle Eastern affairs had cause to be less sanguine. While there was no discernible pattern in the individual happenings of half a dozen not very stable societies, each had the potential for creating trouble. It was disconcerting, for example, to hear the Israeli Prime Minister, Yitzhak Shamir, announce in early January to his Likud bloc that the "big immigration" to Israel of Soviet Jews "requires Israel to be big as well." The occupied territories of the West Bank and Gaza would be needed, he said, "to house the people." In effect, Israel was announcing its intention to remain in the occupied areas. The State Department, with its habitual capacity for diplomatic understatement, thought the Prime Minister's remarks "not helpful."

So, also, in Kuwait, a quite different "crisis" presented itself; thousands of peaceful pro-democracy demonstrators, marching to protest the dissolution of the National Assembly in 1986 and demanding the restoration of parliamentary rule, were dispersed by the police with tear gas and water cannons. An event of less than cosmic importance, it confirmed what many Middle East experts knew: even in one of the least populated of the Arab states, where indescribable oil riches were supposed to create universal satisfaction, there was disconcerting evidence of dangerous disaffection.

While Lebanon had fallen from the front pages of American newspapers, particularly after President Reagan's removal of all American troops, the crisis in that country continued unabated. New outbreaks of violence, drawing on tensions between Muslim and Christian military forces, created additional threats to frequently announced and habitually violated cease-fires. Syrian and Iranian forces remained active in the country, and the future of Lebanon was more in doubt in 1990 than it had been when President Bush entered the White House.

Meanwhile, in Iraq, in an incident that did not touch the United States directly, an Iranian-born British free-lance correspondent, Farzard Bazoft, was accused of espionage and sentenced to death. Despite pleas from the British and others for clemency, Bazoft was executed; Britain retaliated by recalling its ambassador. Such events, characteristic of Iraqi politics, received little attention in the United States. Not so, however, with the announcement on April 2 by Saddam Hussein that Iraq possessed advanced chemical weapons, that half of Israel would be destroyed if that country dared to launch a preemptive strike against Iraq's chemical facilities. Margaret Tutwiler, the spokesperson for the State Department, declared: "We have seen these reports, and if they are true, what we have seen is inflammatory, irresponsible, and outrageous." The words were strong. No action flowed from them. Saddam was a man known for his threats; it was all Arab rhetoric. In the four months that followed, no American policy modification was made to suggest that Saddam's words merited something more than public rebuke.

Indeed, there was much more interest in the traditional issues that concerned the mass media, principally violence in the Israeli-occupied areas. For more serious observers of the Jerusalem scene, the failure of Shimon Peres to form a government and the success of Shamir in reconstituting his own government, gaining the support of several small religious parties known to be hostile to negotiations with the Palestinians, suggested that the Baker plan to initiate negotiations between Israel and its Arab neighbors would have to be put on hold. More than ever, Shamir appeared adamant in his refusal to accept an early negotiation along the lines suggested by the Americans, which would almost certainly require Israel to leave the occupied territories. The mass protests of young Palestinians in the streets continued; the American media gave increasing attention to the almost daily violent encounters between rock-throwing Arab youths and Israel's military forces.

In early July the Iranian and Iraqi Foreign Ministers met in Geneva for their first direct talks since the end of their war in 1988. Both expressed optimism that a permanent peace settlement was possible. Again, the event was of capital importance, but to an administration that paid more heed to relations between Israel and Jordan than to relations between Iran and Iraq, such developments were little reflected on. More significant, from Washington's perspective, was the meeting between the Syrian President and the Egyptian President, in which Assad announced his readiness to join in the Arab-Israeli peace process. This was an event that resonated for an administration concerned overwhelmingly with Arab-Israeli relations.

Yet, in the last two weeks of July, any number of incidents occurred that ought to have told both the President and his Secretary of State that the situation in the Middle East was suddenly precarious, that something quite out of the ordinary was happening. Neither recognized this, though both must have seen that the diplomatic comings and goings had become substantially more frenetic. Saddam Hussein, on July 17, delivered a speech highly critical of the Arab Persian Gulf nations, charging them with "plotting" to hold down oil prices. On July 18, Saddam sent a letter to the Arab League claiming that Kuwait was stealing oil from the disputed Rumaila oil field, which straddled the two countries. Coincidental with this message came a demand from Iraq's Foreign Minister, Tariq Aziz, that Iraq's $30 billion debt to its Arab neighbors be written off. Aziz, flying to Cairo for discussions with Hosni Mubarak, was joined there by the King of Jordan. Egypt's President, appreciating the gravity of what was told him in these meetings, decided to visit Kuwait, Iraq, and Saudi Arabia at once. For him, the Iraqi threats were substantially more serious than they appeared to be to those who viewed them from the distance of Washington. It was significant, then, that he announced, with obvious relief and satisfaction, that the Iraqis and the Kuwaitis had agreed to hold talks in Jidda, Saudi Arabia, to discuss their differences. Scheduled for August 1, the talks in fact broke down after a single two-hour session.

It is inconceivable, given the quality of America's diplomatic representation in Cairo, that the United States did not have full information on the nature of all the discussions that involved Mubarak. While April Glaspie, Ambassador to Iraq, may never have understood the import of Saddam's words and sought only to explain her own President, showing how he too suffered at the hands of the American media, assuring the President of Iraq that he need not take too seriously their criticism of his policies, equivalent ineptness and indiscretion was not likely with Frank Wisner, the United States Ambassador to Egypt, who understood the Egyptian interest in the Iraq-Kuwait struggle perfectly. The White House had ample warning of Saddam's threats and capabilities, if not from its own ambassador in Baghdad, then from other sources, including, most importantly, Israeli intelligence. The mistakes were made not only by a well-meaning ambassador, who could claim some distinction as an Arab specialist, but at the highest levels by an administration that could never take Iraq seriously. It was, after all, just one more of those radical grubby Arab states that merited no special attention. The State Department's later efforts to distance itself from its ambassador in Baghdad, to make April Glaspie's errors appear wholly her own, showed a characteristic lack of bureaucratic honesty.

The failure to attend to Iraq during eight years of war, and in the first year and a half of the Bush administration as well, showed a blindness common to a government dominated by men who knew only one version of history, who were following a Nixon-period script they barely understood. In seeking to rekindle the more aggressive Middle Eastern diplomatic policies initiated by Kissinger and pursued under Presidents Nixon and Ford, hoping finally to bring to fruition negotiations successfully concluded by President Carter at Camp David, they failed to recognize how much the geopolitical conditions in the area had changed. A more supple group might have wished to construct an agenda more suited to 1989 and 1990, one that took account of the collapse of the Soviet Union and considered how the military ambitions of both Iraq and Iran might be affected. The administration's concerns with Arab grievances in the occupied territories were reasonable, if placed in a broader context. The failure of both the President and his Secretary of State to interest themselves in Iran—to seek some sort of political relation with that once friendly state—was exceeded only by their innocence in not knowing how to deal with Iraq, a desperate state, economically and ideologically bankrupt, and therefore militarily unstable.

In the end, they could take none of these things seriously enough; Teheran and Baghdad could not compete for the attention of men whose minds were fixed on Moscow and Bonn, real powers, nations with whom important business could be conducted. But the death of Marxism—if it was that, a dubious proposition at best—did not coincide with the death of nationalism; indeed, it only contributed to its growth. Oblivious to this, the President and his Secretary of State deluded themselves about the nature of the world they were seeking to refashion. To have coped with its new possibilities would have required them to command intellectual resources they lacked, economic capital that lay hidden, if it existed at all, and a political will that took into account certain fundamental ideological and geopolitical realities that had not existed in the time of the Shah or of Brezhnev.

The invasion that took place on August 2 could not have been averted by a more able or more adequately instructed American ambassador in Baghdad. If Saddam misled his Arab colleagues as well—a claim many times repeated by Mubarak —it is unlikely that an American would have learned very much of his final intentions from speaking with him, or would then have been able to get the President to counter his threats. In August 1990, the President showed himself an accomplished actor. No longer having to worry about Soviet intransigence or interference, his United Nations Ambassador went to the Security Council in full confidence that it would condemn the invasion and order an immediate Iraqi withdrawal. The possibility of a Soviet veto was nil, given Gorbachev's desperate need for American support to make at all credible his own very fragile hold on power.

The Security Council vote of August 6, introducing a system of sanctions, followed by the decision by King Fahd of Saudi Arabia to request military assistance from the United States, allowed for the rapid dispatch of 2,300 American paratroopers and AWACS, B-52, and F-111 aircraft. The British, responding to a similar plea from the Saudi monarch, agreed to send their own air and naval units into the Gulf. While the United States insisted that its troop deployments were "wholly defensive," Egyptian President Mubarak recognized the problems created by what, in his eyes, was a too overt Western military intervention. His initial hope was that Egypt might participate in a joint Arab "umbrella" force to facilitate Iraq's withdrawal from Kuwait. If the Arab states could work together to persuade Saddam to withdraw from Kuwait, Mubarak's own position in Egypt would be substantially improved and his reputation in the whole Arab world enhanced. He failed in his efforts. While twelve of the twenty-one member nations of the Arab League agreed to send troops to Saudi Arabia, to assist in her defense, the others rejected the proposal.

Very early, Bush perceived several possibilities. Knowing with some degree of accuracy, and not only from intelligence sources, what the Iraqi military capabilities were—the United States had contributed to creating them, along with other NATO allies—it is possible that he estimated them at their real worth. If Saddam Hussein, under whatever pretext, agreed to leave, the President was certain to emerge as the hero who had organized United Nations opposition to him. If Saddam remained, additional forces would be mobilized. The American military equipment and manpower necessary for Gulf operations could be rapidly transferred from Europe, where they were no longer needed, and from bases in the United States. The timing for a risk-free political and military action was perfect. Still, for the President to succeed, caution was imperative. To rouse suspicions prematurely about his objectives would kindle a domestic public debate that could prove deleterious to his designs.

On August 9, the Security Council declared Iraq's annexation of Kuwait "null and void." That same day, King Fahd termed the Iraqi invasion a "vile aggression," and Saddam called for a "holy war"—a jihad—against "aggressive invaders," linking them to the "disfigured petroleum states." Castigating the "invaders" from without and the "profligate and rich" from within, for whom true Arabs could never have any sympathy, Saddam began to invent the political scenario that he expected would bring protesting Arabs into the streets of a hundred cities. As the authentic voice of Islamic pride, seeking to advance the claims of Arabs unjustly dispossessed of their lands, he spoke to all who felt themselves humiliated, the victims of Western imperialism, Zionist aggression, and American yearning for world domination. Those who opposed him would be ground into the earth; they would never succeed in their foul designs. The Iraqi dictator spoke to the world of Islam; the President spoke to the world.

As early as August 10, administration officials began to speak of the possibility that United States troop levels in the region would reach 100,000 in a matter of months. American naval units, after August 16, took up their stations in the Gulf, in touch with other Coalition forces sent to enforce the sanctions voted by the United Nations. Saddam shocked the Western world with his unexpected announcement that 3,000 Americans and 5,000 Europeans, in Kuwait and Iraq at the time the troubles began, would not be allowed to leave. Hostages, in numbers never previously conceived of, were suddenly seen to be at the mercy of Iraq's dictator. The American President, from his Kennebunkport vacation retreat, condemned what he saw as an unspeakable act of barbarism.

The American interest, riveted on the hostages, a subject made familiar from a decade of attention given to hostage taking in Iran and Lebanon, reflected a growing fascination with the diabolical actions of a man who did what civilized nations never thought to do. The history of Saddam's crimes became prime-time news; the Kurds were rediscovered, the Democrats having tried in vain to draw attention to them just days before the invasion. When, on August 17, Saddam announced that the Westerners were Iraq's "guests," that they would be distributed to strategic points throughout the country, protecting Iraq against the aggression of outsiders, this was considered the ultimate outrage, a barbarism unknown to history. The leader who had murdered innumerable colleagues, killed Kurds and others, and used poison gas against tens of thousands of Iranian soldiers, not to speak of the indignities he inflicted on Shiites in Iraq, was seen for what he was, a human monster.

Although the invasion of Kuwait came as a surprise, the President, as usual, appeared calm and unperturbed. In his press conference of August 8, asked whether American intelligence "had let us down," he responded with a hearty "not at all." As he explained, in contradiction of facts known to several Arab and other foreign offices, there had been no intelligence failure; in his words, "when you plan a blitzkrieg-like attack that's launched at two in the morning, it's pretty hard to stop, particularly when you have just been given the word of the people involved that there wouldn't be any such attack." The President, having spoken, left for Maine. He would not allow himself to be imprisoned in the White House in the way poor Jimmy Carter had been by the Iran hostage taking. On August 28, to the great relief of many, Saddam announced that all Western women and children held hostage in Iraq would be released. The American buildup continued.

Secretary of State Baker, visiting King Fahd in Jidda on September 6, made his first plea for financial aid. The role Saudi Arabia had once willingly assumed for Iraq, agreeing to be its banker, it was now prepared to perform for the greatest military power in the world, regrettably an economic pauper (of sorts). The Saudi king, acknowledging America's need, and understanding the federal government's budgetary problems and the President's determination not to meet exceptional defense expenses by raising new taxes or borrowing, agreed to provide $500 million a month to help support the American military deployments in the Gulf. An additional Saudi pledge, of some $4 billion in aid to various Third World countries adversely affected by the war, was warmly welcomed by the President's emissary.

Baker, meeting also with the exiled emir of Kuwait, who had taken refuge in Saudi Arabia, received a second promise of financial assistance; this time, $3 billion was offered to help offset the exceptional expenses being incurred by the United States. In effect, two oil-rich Arab states, one already occupied and the other fearing invasion, both incapable of self-defense, agreed to contribute militarily what they could, recognizing, however, that a financial contribution would also be necessary. To say that the American troops had become "mercenaries," fighting for Arab states prepared to pay for their keep, was too harsh. Still, if the war, thought to be impending, was not to be seen in that light, with the United States having taken the place of Iraq as the beneficiary of Saudi and Kuwaiti largesse, other "bankers" had to be brought in.

Securing additional funds, and not only from rich Arab states, became a political and diplomatic imperative. Japan, one of the industrial societies almost wholly dependent on Gulf oil, was a prime candidate for a large solicitation. Because the United States preened itself on defending Japan's interests— though no explicit request was made for such a defense, Japan believing always that it could have accomplished that objective in other ways—a large Japanese contribution was expected. Again, a financial subsidy seemed entirely appropriate, at least to Americans who knew something of the size of Japan's national purse. The original amount pledged by the Japanese was thought to be derisory; after considerable and not very subtle pressure, it was raised, but never to a figure that many Americans thought adequate. The Japanese constitution, framed by the Americans after World War II, prohibited a military involvement. Money was all Japan could give, and many in Congress felt it was giving too little.

They were equally unhappy with Germany's contribution. Again, constitutional restraints precluded the dispatch of military forces, and West Germany pledged $2 billion to the common effort. Because West Germany was investing heavily in Eastern Europe and in East Germany, this was considered, at least by the Bonn government, to be a significant financial commitment. Americans disposed to think about the matter at all were unimpressed; by their reckoning, the sums offered both by Japan and by Germany were woefully inadequate.

Meanwhile, in view of the nature of the crisis, an extraordinary summit meeting of the Presidents of the United States and the Soviet Union seemed to be called for. For seven hours, in Helsinki, on September 9, Bush and Gorbachev met together to discuss the Gulf situation. In their joint statement, they condemned Iraq for invading Kuwait and demanded an immediate and unconditional withdrawal. At the same time, the United States explicitly recognized the Soviet interest in Arab-Israeli peace efforts, and implied that there would be a place for the USSR in any international negotiations on the subject. While the press conference statements suggested subtle but undefined differences in the American and Soviet interpretations of how Saddam might best be treated, Baker, meeting with NATO Foreign Ministers in Brussels after Helsinki, called the Soviets "very reliable partners." Greater praise could not have been uttered. When, on September 11, the President addressed a joint session of Congress, he promised that "Saddam Hussein will fall." This seemed to go considerably beyond any of his earlier pledges, which simply reiterated the American interest in seeing Iraq withdraw from Kuwait, but not much was made of a seemingly innocent remark. The Congress assumed it was the conventional presidential hyperbole.

In New York, a far more momentous statement was made at the United Nations by the Soviet Foreign Minister, Eduard Shevardnadze. He indicated that the Soviet Union would support UN-approved military action against Iraq, if recommended. The Security Council, a day later, voted 14–1 to

extend the embargo of Iraq to include all airborne traffic.
Meanwhile, both Britain and France announced plans to send
additional troops and military equipment to Saudi Arabia. At
the United Nations, addressing the General Assembly, President Bush implied that the Iraqi pullout from Kuwait might
provide the opportunity "to settle conflicts that divide the Arabs
from Israel." In Turtle Bay, this was a reasonable thing for
him to say. It committed the United States to no specific policy,
but indicated in a place where Arabs were powerful the
American interest in an early settlement of the Palestinian
problem.

These events preoccupied the country during the days of
September. Meanwhile, in Washington, a news story appeared
in *The Washington Post* that led the Secretary of Defense to
dismiss General Michael Dugan, the chief of the Air Force,
who had spoken with rare candor about American military
plans for an attack on Iraq if Saddam Hussein persisted in
refusing to leave Kuwait. While Secretary Dick Cheney and
the Chairman of the Joint Chiefs of Staff, General Colin Powell,
were said to be angered by the military information divulged
and by the claims made for the role the Air Force would play
in any operation against Iraq, there were more fundamental
reasons for their displeasure. General Dugan revealed what no
American was supposed to say, that Iraq was, in effect, a "paper
tiger," a term he chose not to use, though he made that point
very explicitly when he said that the Iraqi Air Force "has very
limited capability." But he went further in an interview that
had taken some ten hours during flights to and from Saudi
Arabia. General Dugan said that the Iraqis "did not distinguish
themselves in the war against Iran, often missing targets by
miles." Iraq, he claimed, had "an incompetent army"; if this
was insufficiently explicit, he went on to add: "With 5,000 tanks
one should have been able to do something" against Iran. The
Iraqis, despite their propaganda, were not militarily very able.
The Americans knew this; so did the Israelis. Indeed, the latter
had urged that since Iraq was a one-man show, it made sense

to target Saddam, his family, his personal guard, and his mistress as prime targets. If that "decapitation" occurred, the war would end.

Still, achieving that specific objective might not be easy. There was no guarantee, Dugan said, that "bombers would be able to find Saddam." Dugan expected that air power, however, would so shatter enemy resistance that soldiers could "walk in and not have to fight." The Air Force chief gave the scenario for what in fact happened four months later, even going so far as to suggest that American support for the war would continue "until body bags come home." The President had no intention of the last happening, and his dismissed Air Force chief told the readers of *The Washington Post* why it need not happen. He was relieved from duty for telling the truth, accurately describing plans which emphasized what American air power would achieve, which gave no attention whatever to the military assistance that would come from the Coalition, so ingeniously created by the telephone calls of the President and his ever-traveling Secretary of State.

Meanwhile, the Soviet President, sensitive always to international public opinion, particularly in Europe, persisted in telling his foreign friends what he was doing to persuade a difficult ally to be reasonable and responsible. Press reports in the West suggested that the Soviets were perhaps making some progress in their talks. On October 14, the Soviet news agency Novesti reported that Saddam would be willing to consider a withdrawal from Kuwait in return for the complete control of the Rumaila oil field and two islands at the head of the Persian Gulf. Secretary of State Baker responded at once; no such solution was satisfactory. On the stump, in speeches delivered in support of Republican Party candidates, the President was no less explicit; the only acceptable solution was a complete withdrawal of all Iraqi troops from Kuwait. The public opinion polls registered support for the President in his insistence that aggression reap no rewards.

On October 29, again in response to American initiatives,

the UN Security Council voted 13–0, with 2 abstentions, to declare Iraq liable for all financial losses, injuries, and damages caused by its invasion of Kuwait. On that same day, the Security Council's Military Staff Committee met to discuss the crisis. The Secretary of State visited the Middle East, the Soviet Union, and Western Europe to make certain that all understood America's resolve to make no concessions to Iraq, that all remained committed to the original United Nations resolutions requiring Iraq to depart unconditionally from Kuwait. In Cairo, Baker met with the Chinese Foreign Minister, Qian Qichen, who assured him that China would not use its veto in the Security Council if a resolution was pressed authorizing the use of military force against Iraq. It was assumed that some concessions had been made to the Chinese to assure their cooperation, but this seemed a small price to the President, who by this time had almost certainly concluded that he would have to avail himself of the military option.

The elections safely over, President Bush informed the country on November 8 that the American forces in the Gulf numbered over 200,000, and that he intended to increase them further, to a total of 400,000 by early 1991, to guarantee "an adequate offensive military option." The President neglected to explain why such an offensive capability was necessary. A military force originally introduced for defensive purposes only, to protect Saudi Arabia, with economic sanctions of the most stringent kind approved to compel Iraq to abandon Kuwait, was no longer thought to be sufficient. Congressional leaders, in recess, spoke of returning for a special session to discuss what was recognized to be a major change in White House strategy. In the end, nothing came of this, in part because Congress would have included a number of "lame ducks," members who would not be sitting in the new Congress. Because of the importance of the issue, and the debate it was expected to generate, only the new Congress was thought adequate to a discussion that many believed might lead the United States to war.

The President, visiting with the American troops in Saudi Arabia for Thanksgiving, meeting with both King Fahd and Kuwait's Sheik Jabir, and then going on to meet with President Mubarak in Cairo and Syrian President Assad in Geneva, appeared concerned principally that his Arab allies remain firm in their commitment to his policies. Rarely had a leader of a military alliance in the twentieth century revealed greater nervousness. It was as if the Coalition, a flimsy and delicate construction, to be sure, would not survive any shock. Still, for the President, Arab allies were all-important. Indeed, who they were, what they represented, why they should wish to stand with the United States against Iraq, seemed wholly secondary.

The fact that Assad had been the sworn enemy of Saddam for decades, that he had reasons for wanting Iraq to be defeated militarily, was conveniently forgotten. No one looked at what Assad had been doing in the previous months in Lebanon, where he was asserting increasing control over what had once been an independent republic. All attention was given to keeping the Coalition together, intact and strong. This was the key to more than winning a military engagement against Saddam; the President imagined he would win the hearts and minds of Islam—at least a part of that vast religious community—by creating an alliance that included major Arab members. If Saddam's error was to believe that Muslims would rise in his defense in the Maghreb and elsewhere, Bush made a comparable mistake—he imagined that he was hiring Arab goodwill, that in the long run it would make it easier for him to compel concessions from Israel.

The most important of the UN Security Council resolutions, that of November 29, followed intensive lobbying by the United States. By a vote of 15–0, member states were authorized "to use all means necessary" to bring about an immediate and unconditional Iraqi withdrawal from Kuwait. The resolution gave Iraq until January 15, 1991, to comply; failure to do so would allow the Coalition to move militarily. The American President, having been reassured by his Arab allies of their fidelity, now received a United Nations mandate to use military force after January 15, if necessary. The Iraqi dictator had one of two choices—to leave Kuwait or to be militarily defeated there. Having long calculated the possibility of such a scenario, the President knew he would win, whatever the final choice.

In the circumstances, it was easy for him to make one final offer, inviting the Iraqis to negotiate. While it was never clear what such negotiations would deal with, the Iraqi Foreign Minister was asked to come to Washington to discuss the crisis; the President offered to send his own Secretary of State to Baghdad for the same purpose. Iraq accepted "the idea of the invitation and the meeting," and on December 6 announced that all foreign hostages in Iraq and Kuwait would be liberated. More than 1,000 foreigners began to leave on December 9, and some 2,000 others left in the weeks following. On December 5, the Israeli Foreign Minister warned that Israel might attack Iraq if the United States failed to force a withdrawal from Kuwait and a dismantling of Iraq's military. The United Nations resolutions had never explicitly suggested the latter as a condition of Iraq's compliance with its demands.

On December 14, President Bush indicated that the talks with Iraq were "on hold"; Iraq was asked to agree to receive Secretary Baker no later than January 3, 1991. In the weeks that followed, negotiations continued, concerned chiefly with establishing a mutually satisfactory meeting date. This proved impossible. Saddam insisted on a date later than January 3; Bush refused to hear of it. When Iraq's President proposed a meeting on January 12, this was taken to be a ruse: the Iraqi leader was simply trying to prevent the United States from doing what the United Nations mandate allowed it to do, at any time after January 15. While the clock was running out, France, the European Community, the Secretary-General of the United Nations, and the Soviet Union all thought at one time or other of trying to persuade Saddam to withdraw. Visits to Baghdad became common in these weeks, though the last of these, that of the Secretary-General of the United Nations, indicated that there was no prospect of Iraq's complying with the Security Council's demands.

In this event-laden autumn, the United States was much preoccupied with Saddam, but other events, closer to home, constantly intruded to withdraw attention from the Gulf. Indeed, at times it seemed almost as if the President was as anxious to defeat Congress as he was to wrestle with Iraq's President. The issue, technically, was the federal budget, on which a great deal of time was expended in a bipartisan effort to reduce the deficit. Like so much else in the Bush administration, this became a war of words, conferring an importance on an inconsequential struggle that wholly distorted its intrinsic character. The American people were expected to view the matter gravely. Indeed, the President threatened to close the government down rather than allow a spendthrift Congress to have its way. When the compromise measure was finally rejected in the House by a vote of 254–179, the House and Senate approved a stopgap spending bill, which the President, faithful to his threat, promptly vetoed, confident that his veto would be sustained.

For a number of days, it appeared that the government would indeed be obliged to shut down; a number of facilities, including the Statue of Liberty and other almost equally prominent monuments, as well as national parks, did in fact close. Happily, the main functions of government were spared; they ground on in their traditional fashion. When, after much acrimony, both houses voted a compromise budget, the President agreed to allow two stopgap spending bills, to give both houses additional time to work out details. Congress was able to adjourn finally on October 28, just days before the election, sending several packages to the White House. The President signed thirteen appropriation bills and a deficit reduction package on November 5, two days before the election. He spoke angrily and frequently, as did television commentators, of the sad spectacle provided by Congress, unable to agree on something as crucial as the nation's budget.

If Congress disappointed him in not approving a budget so arduously worked out by bipartisan agreement, it showed itself solidly behind him in consenting to his military buildup in the Gulf. The House of Representatives, by a vote of 380–29, accepted on October 1 a resolution supporting his actions "with respect to Iraqi aggression in Kuwait." The Senate adopted a comparable resolution by a vote of 96–3 the following day. Later in the month, at the President's request, Congress agreed to forgive Egypt its $7 billion debt. Secretary of State Baker, in testimony before the Senate Foreign Relations Committee on October 17 and the House Foreign Affairs Committee on October 18, showed immense self-confidence, resisting any congressional participation or involvement in decision making. Foreign affairs, he insisted, was an executive responsibility; it did not fall within the proper jurisdiction of Congress. With Congress in recess, the President would only say that he would consult Congress if Iraq did not by a sudden provocation bring war on unexpectedly. The term "consult" was intentionally ambiguous.

The new Congress, scheduled to convene on January 3, was expected to make the Gulf a prime order of business just as soon as it organized itself. In the interim, the administration behaved as if presidential authority, sufficient on numerous occasions in the past to justify a decision to dispatch and engage military units, might be called on to do the same again. There was no reason, according to White House sources, to depart from presidential procedures said to have excellent nineteenth- and twentieth-century precedents. In congressional committees, growing criticism by individual Democrats, led in the Senate by Sam Nunn, suggested that the earlier almost automatic approval of the President's actions did not extend to what he now seemed to be planning: a war against Iraq, undertaken before sanctions were allowed to prove their effectiveness. The Senate Armed Services Committee hearings in late November and early December, like those held before the Senate Foreign Relations Committee, showed restiveness, even fear, particularly among Democrats, but these misgivings were insufficient to persuade the Democratic Party leadership to recommend a special session of the Congress.

If senators increasingly hostile to the President's actions fully realized the difficulties they would encounter in a debate likely to occur very close to the January 15 deadline, they nevertheless did nothing to protect themselves. The administration continued to insist that congressional approval was unnecessary; the government, if it took military action, would simply be enforcing the mandates of the Security Council. The Democrats miscalculated badly. When the White House knew that it had the necessary votes, that the President would not be defeated in either the Senate or the House, it accepted the idea that Congress should debate the issue. Patriotic support of "our boys and girls in the Gulf" and sending the right message to Saddam became the standard reason for voting as the President wished. The country was invited to hear a Great Debate. Members were asked to vote on whether to instruct the President to desist from making war, as the UN Security Council vote allowed him to do after January 15, whether to insist that he use only sanctions to stop Saddam.

The Great Debate started on January 10, just five days before the United Nations ultimatum expired. Many who heard all or part of the televised proceedings commented on what they perceived to be its extraordinary quality. It was political drama of the highest order, television anchors said. The quality of the individual interventions, the gravity and solemnity of the occasion, gripped many who watched in their homes. In both houses of Congress, men and women spoke carefully and thoughtfully, insisting they had never participated in a more critical debate, on which so much depended. The times were said to be historic; the nation would never forget them. Because the United Nations had approved the January 15 deadline, each member of Congress was being asked, in effect, whether to go along with the President's plan to make war on Iraq if there was no withdrawal before that date. Would Saddam find Congress solidly supporting the President, or would he be able to delude himself, believing that the American people, like Congress, were divided?

Emotions ran high. Before the first day of the three-day debate was over, informed television and newspaper commentators knew that the President would have his way in both houses, but the excitement was not substantially reduced by that fact alone. Two themes emerged: first, for those who questioned the President's policies and intentions, there was a continuing plea that sanctions be given a chance; for those who supported the President, the plea was made that the Commander in Chief, at a moment of supreme danger, should not be repudiated by Congress. With few exceptions, all expected the war to produce numerous American casualties, and there were constant references to Vietnam. Indeed, that war, more than any other single factor, figured in the argument of those who urged caution, negotiation, restraint. The argument carried little weight with those who insisted that Iraq's aggression must not be rewarded, that an evil dictator should not be appeased.

While it would be unjust to suggest that a debate generally thought to have been "great" was in fact mediocre, that possibility ought at least to be considered. What the "debate" revealed, principally, was the power of the late-twentieth-century presidency and the impotence of Congress. Some of the individual performances were adequate; none took in the fundamental fact of what had happened to the American republic. The President was going to have his war, would win it easily, and would emerge smelling of roses; no one was in a position to stop him from doing what he intended; the war would resolve nothing. All the major problems, foreign and domestic, that existed before the fighting began would exist also in the years that followed victory.

Speakers of both parties rose instead to proclaim that this was the most important day of their lives, of their whole legislative careers, that no issue brought before them was so fraught with potential danger. The calculated effort on the part of those who planned the war, and who had been propagandizing for it over many months, making it seem more important and infinitely more hazardous than it could ever be, produced the intended results. Specious arguments were made and believed. No one rose to suggest that every time Congress voted a major appropriation intended to affect the social fabric of the nation, it was acting on a matter as important as the one that led Senators Nunn, Byrd, Pell, Boren, Mitchell, and Levin to propose to require the President "to give sanctions a chance." The resolution, framed in such a way as to suggest no major difference with the President, let alone the brave men and women sent to the Gulf, insisted on keeping alive "the economic and diplomatic pressures against Iraq," but also the "military options," while asking also "for efforts to increase the military and financial contributions made by allied nations." The Democrats had chosen their line of attack; faithful citizens of the country, they wished to do nothing to embarrass the President, let alone harm brave Americans, but their principal concern was to insist that the President had changed his game plan after November 8, when he moved from a defensive stance to one that allowed him to take the offensive. This, in their view, was a grave mistake.

In taking this line, and particularly in dwelling on the extent to which the President, ably abetted by his Secretary of State, had attempted to prevent the American Congress from voting on a resolution to go to war—pretending that there had been two hundred occasions in the past when American Presidents had taken military action without such explicit congressional assent—they failed to take into account that the President

altered his policy and agreed to a full-scale debate only when
he expected, on the basis of what his aides reported to him,
that Congress would in fact go along with him, would not
agree to the resolution that bore the names of a small group
of distinguished Democratic senators. The President encouraged Congress to proceed with its palaver—which it would
have done in any circumstance—when he understood that a
sufficient number of Democrats would support him in both
houses, giving him the majority votes he sought. The President
knew the debate was for the record only; it would change
nothing.

The occasion was remarkable, a golden opportunity for
Democrats and Republicans alike to speak to the nation, to
develop and propagate principles more important than those
that conventionally figured in the daily television talk shows.
Both parties failed in this task; neither house showed itself a
safe haven for men and women prepared to move away from
well-worn argument. The President was going to have his war.
Why not acknowledge that? There was no need to estimate the
casualties precisely; no one could know such a thing. Still, a
military force created to deter or defeat a Soviet attack in
Europe, largely transferred for use in the Middle East to deter
or defeat a third-rate power incapable of winning an eight-
year war against a single Middle Eastern adversary, was likely
to prove more than adequate for the purposes the President
intended, a quick and decisive victory, in the manner of the
Falklands, which would proclaim what the world knew—the
United States was militarily superior to Iraq; the Soviet Union
was incapable of assisting its old Middle Eastern clients. Politics
required the President to pretend that the war had a more
cosmic importance. The United States was confirming its role
as the defender of international law, prepared to risk all in the
cause of principle. Diplomacy required his allies to indulge him
in his fantasies, showing at the same time, by their discreet
silence, solicitude for a fallen economic entity, the Soviet Union,
still recognized to be a formidable thermonuclear power.

# War and Peace

---

I n the beginning was the word, and the word came out of Baghdad. It came, of course, on television, interrupting regularly scheduled evening news programs in the East to announce that the long-awaited United States bombardment of Baghdad had begun. The war was on; it became official a few hours later when the President addressed the nation and the world (mostly still in bed, asleep), giving the speech that could have been written for him days before. The United States, its patience exhausted, together with its Coalition allies, had begun the military campaign that would force the Iraqis to leave Kuwait. The message was clear: the President was doing what Neville Chamberlain had failed to do, what others in the 1930s should have done to stop a mad German dictator. The United States and its loyal allies had no choice but to attack; Marlin Fitzwater, speaking for the President immediately after the bombings began, put it all very succinctly: "The liberation of Kuwait has begun."

The attacks on targets in both Iraq and Kuwait came wholly from the air, from bombers dispatched from unidentified bases and cruise missiles launched from naval ships in the area.

Within hours, the happy news was broadcast that not a single American bomber had been lost. While Saddam, by radio, summoned his people to take up arms and announced the start of the "mother of all battles," denouncing the President as a "hypocritical criminal," the President, comfortable in his role as Commander in Chief, was considerably more calm. His goal, he explained, was "not the conquest of Iraq, it is the liberation of Kuwait." The object, he said, was to knock out Saddam's nuclear bomb potential, while also destroying his chemical weapons facilities. The Secretary of Defense, speaking later in the evening, emphasized that everything possible was being done to avoid civilian targets. Because the Iraqi response had been so limited, some analysts believed that Iraq's air force had already been destroyed. Still, Secretary Cheney cautioned against excessive optimism; in his words, the war "is likely to run for a long period of time." All, however, was going according to plan.

American television had its new entertainment, and Americans an engrossing new war. In the days that followed, and not only on Cable News Network, anchorpersons enjoyed their finest hours. Their reports were interminable, and when photo opportunities were either limited or denied, they relied on the old cast of "experts," former high military and civilian officials or former residents of the region, to explain it all; the new stars were the military briefers in the Pentagon, the networks' own correspondents in the Middle East, and the U.S. commanders in the field. If General Norman Schwarzkopf had not become a household name in the five months leading up to the military assault, he rapidly became that in the five days that followed the attack. In his military garb, the battle uniform that made him, a four-star general, look very much like the man next door preparing a barbecue, Schwarzkopf showed the sangfroid expected of an American military officer who never doubted how the whole affair would end.

It is impossible to exaggerate the extent to which the nation became transfixed by what it saw on television. The film of bursts of antiaircraft fire suggested little about the destruction occurring on the ground, but it provided a fitting background for the charts that explained what the F-117 Stealth fighter-bombers, together with the F-15E bombers, not to speak of other United States aircraft and missiles, were thought to be accomplishing. Though the air attacks were obviously over-whelmingly American, it was constantly emphasized that this was a Coalition war, and the Pentagon made certain that the British and Saudi Tornado fighter-bombers were mentioned, along with the Saudi F-15s and various Kuwaiti bombers. The world was witnessing an unprecedented display of high-tech military capability, carried out by a Coalition created by the diplomatic efforts of the President of the United States and his able Secretary of State.

All the major American players in the nation's capital—except for the Secretary of State, who remained discreetly in the background—had their war television debuts on the very first night of the fighting. General Colin Powell, Chairman of the Joint Chiefs of Staff, at his own news conference, reported that there had been no Iraqi air resistance; others in the Pentagon added essential details. The Iraqi planes were being searched for in their hardened shelters; Scud batteries, capable of reaching Saudi Arabia and Israel, were being valiantly attacked and presumably destroyed. The mood was one of controlled elation; it was D-Day all over again, without the casualties and nothing like the disgraceful war conducted in Vietnam, where the American military were obliged to fight under constraints that made their victory impossible, dogged by a press corps that made the slaughter and the failure vivid to those at home. The shame of Vietnam was at last going to be removed; Americans would again be able to stand tall.

Twenty-four hours later, the euphoria, though scarcely abated in Washington and still growing throughout the country, was considerably less obvious in Israel. Saddam launched Scud missile attacks on both Israel and Saudi Arabia. While only a single Iraqi missile was fired at the Saudis, happily destroyed by an American Patriot antimissile rocket, at least seven, all carrying conventional warheads, landed in Israel, in Tel Aviv and Haifa. There were no reports of Israeli deaths from the Scud missile attacks, but casualties were suffered. Again, happily, it seemed that the missiles did not carry the dreaded poison gas warheads so touted as Saddam's most dangerous weapon. The United States, fearful always for the stability of its fragile Coalition, begged the Israelis not to retaliate. To do so would only complicate American strategy; if the war assumed the character of being essentially a battle between two great military forces on one side—those of the United States and Israel—against Iraq, the other Arab states might withdraw their armies and air forces, or at least threaten to do so. Though the Israelis reserved the right to attack from the second day of the war, the President and his emissaries urged them to be patient and not upset plans so carefully and elaborately worked out, that had brought Saudi Arabia, Egypt, Syria, and Kuwait into a great international Coalition, all pledged to force Iraq to leave Kuwait.

While the administration continued to warn that the war would be long and difficult—an argument calculated to make its victory seem all the greater once it was achieved quickly and at almost no cost in American lives—the New York stock market recognized the true situation and reacted accordingly. Within a day of the initial bombings, oil prices dropped more than $10 a barrel—the largest single-day drop in history—and the Dow Jones average rose a healthy 114 points. Though historians could say, correctly, that war often encouraged new investment and created bull markets, rarely did stock markets register such very large gains. If the stock market rise could be ascribed to war fever in the United States and pride in the efficiency of its remarkable military technology, Saddam's attack on Israel and his continuing fulminations against "the Satan in the White House" raised the question whether rhetoric and ill-targeted bombs, falling indiscriminately on Israel, could defeat America's well-conceived diplomatic and military initiatives, not to speak of its "smart bombs." The television anchors and reporters, working around the clock, could not avoid sounding notes of measured optimism. The American audience for the President's speech on January 16 had been the largest in history; CNN had come of age, rivaling all the other networks because it provided what the public craved—war news twenty-four hours a day.

By Saturday, the beginning of the weekend, America's restaurants and movie houses were deserted—men and women much preferred to stay at home to watch the war. But the news seemed somewhat less encouraging. Iraq's attacks on Israel were continuing; while American air bombardments had destroyed many of the stationary missile launchers from which Iraqi Scuds might have been fired, it was exceedingly difficult to discover and destroy all the mobile launchers. The graphic pictures, cleared by Israeli censorship, of destruction in a heavily populated area of Tel Aviv told the Bush administration that Israel might not tolerate such attacks for very long; patience was beginning to wear thin in Jerusalem, and a major Israeli counterattack could no longer be excluded. Those who knew administration thinking best expressed the hope that such an unfortunate Israeli response—unnecessary and inimical to America's interests—would not lead any of the Arab states to desert the Coalition.

General Schwarzkopf, in one of his first briefings, told of the efforts being made from the air to discover the mobile launchers. A review of American air losses in the first seventy-two hours of combat indicated that eight planes had gone down; the British had lost two, the Italians one, and the Kuwaitis one. Baghdad radio, in its propaganda broadcasts, using the hyperbole it would quickly become famous for, suggested that 94 Allied planes had been brought down. The

American claims of Iraqi air losses were considerably more modest. Though eight had been destroyed in air battles and many were believed to have been shattered on the ground, the greatest part of Iraq's air force had not yet been engaged or destroyed. Where, then, were the 700 Iraqi planes, which had been so much feared before the fighting began? The common wisdom suggested that they had been dispersed to the north, where they were presumably concealed in concrete bunkers. Was Allied intelligence, certainly helped by Israeli intelligence, unable to detect their whereabouts? Such embarrassing questions were never put. The major television broadcasts, emphasizing principally Iraq's attacks on Israel—missiles flew splendidly even through bad weather—gave some heed also to other, less obviously crucial war news. Thus, for example, reports told of the enthusiasm registered in Amman, Jordan, for what fellow Arabs in Iraq were finally doing to Zionist Israel.

Sunday was a harsh day for those who stayed at home to watch the war on television. Iraq used the Christian Sabbath to display on Baghdad television seven Allied airmen shot down: three Americans, two Britons, a Kuwaiti, and an Italian. In their blurred representations of these unfortunate men, they deeply alarmed an American viewing public unprepared for such cruel and uncivilized behavior. One of the American prisoners, identified as Warrant Officer Guy Hunter, Jr., was heard to say: "I think the war is crazy and should never have happened. I condemn this aggression against peaceful Iraq." Other comments of the same kind told Pentagon officials that the prisoners had been forced to speak in this way; Iraq's mistreatment of prisoners of war was barbarous; civilized nations did not comport themselves in this way. Iraq's chargé d'affaires, who had remained in Washington, was called in by the State Department to be told that the United States would hold Iraq responsible for violating the Geneva Convention. American television spoke in more passionate terms: Saddam

Hussein was a beast who did not play by the accepted rules of war.

By the weekend, the idea that this might be another six-day war, rather like the one Israel fought decades earlier against Egypt, Syria, and Jordan, was dashed. The Bush administration, because of its political interests, had never suggested that possibility, but in the first excited hours after the initial bombardments, less cautious citizens entertained the idea of a very short war. The President and his advisers preferred to dwell on Iraq's daunting military capability, obviously greatly reduced, but still very considerable. Also, it was impossible to ignore the fighting record of its formidable Republican Guards. No one in an official position suggested an imminent end to the fighting; no one hazarded a guess on when Saddam would throw in the towel.

In the extensive television coverage, which almost always skirted that issue, certain facts were constantly emphasized. First, the return of very hot weather in the Gulf, expected by late March or early April, and the imminent beginning of the Islamic holy season of Ramadan, suggested that the Allies would do well to hasten their military operations. Though they probably could not do more in the air—bad weather was said to be seriously hampering those operations—television's persistent question was whether a major ground offensive was being contemplated and when that might begin. Common wisdom said that it could not be too long delayed, though all agreed that a softening up of Iraq's armies from the air was absolutely essential. Television's technology and its preponderant concern to give the war a powerful ongoing pictorial presentation guaranteed that it would cover the "story" day by day, depending on its talk shows to communicate shifts in Washington thinking about the merits of various military strategies. For more serious reflection, uninterrupted by the need to air commercials, the few American newspapers that retained some reputation for news reporting and editorial

comment enjoyed a slight advantage. While they could never
hope to compete with a medium determined to suggest that
every moment was pregnant with happening and that one must
never risk being too distant from the television screen, the
print media provided a more sustained commentary on the
likely prospects of an air war that was damaging Iraq but was
unlikely, by itself, to force Saddam to surrender.

As early as January 20, *The New York Times*, quoting Pentagon
sources, reported that after three days of "one of the most
intensive air campaigns in the history of warfare," it was clear
that air power alone would not suffice to force Saddam to leave
Kuwait. A ground attack against Iraq's Republican Guards
would almost certainly be required. While the United States
could claim to have gained air superiority over much of Iraq,
and had presumably destroyed a great deal on the ground, all
of Iraq's air defenses had not been destroyed; its mobile missile
launchers could still threaten Scud attacks on targets in both
Saudi Arabia and Israel. In a front-page article that bore the
headline "U.S. War Plan: Still the Ground to Conquer," one
unnamed Pentagon source was quoted as saying: "Everybody
is down on his knees hoping these guys will break," but it was
considered unlikely; a ground campaign would be required.
That message came to be increasingly conveyed in the days
that followed.

While many grieved over the insult done the nation through
the exhibiting of its downed airmen, unfortunate prisoners of
war, and while television remained fixated on the Gulf War,
events were also occurring elsewhere in the world. Neither the
President nor his principal advisers gave these happenings
much heed; if they did, they gave them scant public notice.
Again, the difference between the news disseminated by the
people's medium—commercial and cable television—and that
available to the more restricted audiences who continued to
consult the few quality newspapers and magazines that survive, could not have been more apparent. Television had

become the favored mistress of both the White House and the Pentagon. The priorities set by the President and those few he chose to consult determined what the general public was supposed to know about the war and, more importantly, what it was supposed to be interested in.

Not the least of the services performed by the nation's print media was to make the war its primary concern while retaining some residual respect for the fact that the rest of the world went on as well and did not wholly center on President Bush, Secretary Cheney, and Generals Powell and Schwarzkopf. Indeed, these newspapers and magazines, even in their treatment of the war, showed a freedom from White House direction that television rarely sought and almost never achieved. Thus, for example, while *The New York Times* gave more than ample attention to war news—reporting on what the arrival of Patriot missiles in Israel did to moderate opinion in that sorely tried nation, on why, even after the destruction of the basic services in Baghdad, including power and water, the city remained defiant, on how the continued fear of terrorism in the United States had mobilized the FBI—it also found room, in a conspicuous place, on page one, for a story from Kaunas, Lithuania. That republic did not much figure in the Sunday television talk shows, where only the desert merited close and continuous scrutiny.

Television's obsession with the war had caused it to become a sort of visual tabloid, particularly when it reported news likely to cause grief or discomfort among those who felt most keenly the tragedy of the POWs. The bathos generated through an interview in which a known television personality questioned the distraught parents of an American airman captured by Iraq showed such insensitivity that one could only wonder why the medium had been so wholly captured by the maudlin. Human interest stories, thought legitimate for public airing, reeked of sentimentality, and obscured the devastation occurring on the ground, both in Iraq and in Kuwait. With the exception of CNN, perhaps, which the administration reviled and almost constantly criticized for its loose-cannon reporting out of Baghdad, there was little that reflected independent judgment in the television reporting, though each commercial network sought to outdo the other in its efforts to prove itself original. Still, a form of self-censorship developed, guaranteeing that no really outrageous liberties were taken. No television producer, for example, thought it expedient or necessary in the first days of the conflict, to interview the parents of an Iraqi child maimed or killed in a bombing raid in Baghdad. That was not thought to be news; in any case, arranging that sort of interview would have been more difficult. Most importantly, it would not have served the nation's war purposes.

Television's interviews with high-ranking Allied military officers—CNN, in its conspicuous tolerance, had time for all, even the British commanders—provided an additional news resource, thought very valuable in the beginning. Only much later did the media begin to complain that their access to news was in fact being restricted, that they were not being told all, not being granted access to colonels who knew more than they did, and were being denied entry to military stations that would have helped them understand United States strategy and intentions. Did the administration not trust them to be responsible? Were they less concerned to protect American lives than all other good patriotic Americans?

The complaints were familiar; they had figured frequently both in Vietnam and in Korea; indeed, the American historian might say that they originated even earlier, in the nineteenth century, during the Civil War. In this instance, they had particular poignancy, since they confused a real problem with a false one. It was not so much that the American media were being denied information, that their news diet, fed and strictly controlled by the military, was too meager; rather, the media had been co-opted, taken in, enlisted. They had been skillfully guided into communicating precisely the story the administration wished to disseminate. While Congress had failed to see the President's true intentions before January 15, the media failed catastrophically to do so in the weeks that followed.

The White House depended on communicating a single tale: the war would be difficult; only ingenious American military and political planning could cause it to be brief, and, no less importantly, virtually casualty-free. So long as the media accepted the idea that only White House intelligence and resolve prevented Saddam Hussein from causing a massacre among the Coalition forces assembled to contain him, they contributed in creating the myth that the President and his close advisers wished them to communicate. Even experienced observers were vulnerable to the administration's plans to co-opt the media, as exemplified by the case of James Reston, an accomplished reporter, once the "dean" of Washington correspondents. Reston, long retired from *The New York Times*, occasionally left his island retreat to visit his old haunts, to write a *Times* column. He considered it particularly important to do so in periods of national peril. For him, the Gulf War qualified as that.

Having visited the nation's capital, presumably to discuss the war with those who knew the situation, Reston sat down to communicate what he had learned, to give advice to the President as only very great journalists—men like Walter Lippman, too long dead—frequently did. What, then, did he choose to say? First, that the United States would do well not to accommodate Saddam Hussein, not to fight on the battlefield of his choice. As Reston explained, a ground offensive would see American soldiers fighting on terrain "familiar to his troops and unfamiliar to ours." Reston's first advice was thus to steer clear of a ground war if at all possible; it was too dangerous. He could not understand why the Bush administration did not simply aim its "smart bombs" at the Iraqi dictator himself; the tactic was certainly justified if it saved American lives.

Reston worried that the U.S. Army and Marines, lacking

Eisenhower's "courage of patience," might be pressing for a battle, seeking to prove themselves as efficient as the Air Force and the Navy; he hoped the President would resist such pressures, realizing it was not in the American interest to make Iraq a wasteland, opening it to "Iran's and Syria's tender mercies." Reston's preferred strategy was to make the Iraqi Army surrender not through a great United States victory on the battlefield, which would inevitably produce many American casualties, but through a steady and slow process of attrition, which involved the destruction of the enemy's communications systems and the starvation of its embattled forces. In short, his advice was to carry on the bombings, knowing that they were having an effect on Iraqi soldiers dug into their miserable holes. Reston informed the President that a bloody land war was not in his political interest; that the once senior Washington correspondent of *The New York Times* felt obliged to give such advice showed how little he understood the President, how much he believed, as others once did, that the President was a dim man, who would not know his own political interests.

Reston had fallen squarely into the administration's well-laid trap. The President had no plan to enter into a dangerous ground war, precisely because he knew that it would not be as dangerous as he, for his own political purposes, pretended, and as others, out of their ideological innocence, imagined. The President's estimates of Iraq's military capabilities were considerably more accurate than those provided Reston by his old Washington friends, people who had long abandoned the Pentagon and whose memories were frozen in military categories relevant to Korea and Vietnam but without validity for the Gulf. The most poignant of Reston's recommendations was contained in a single sentence. He wrote: "A bloody land war is not likely to increase his [Bush's] standing in the polls or usher in his new world order, which is more likely to rely on what happens in the Soviet Union than in Iraq and Kuwait."

The fact that Reston failed to perceive the President's military strategy was understandable; like so many other Americans, he lived in a world shaped by Vietnam. The fact that he so totally misconstrued the President's intentions about his so-called new world order—that he could take those empty words seriously—showed a more fundamental flaw. Whatever he had learned from years of observing Dwight Eisenhower, John Kennedy, Lyndon Johnson, Richard Nixon, Gerald Ford, Jimmy Carter, and Ronald Reagan, he recalled not at all when he came to write about George Bush. He understood nothing of the President's intellectual lethargy, nothing of his political ambition. He failed to recognize how decades of service in the Cold War had shaped the man, making him incapable of imagining other than what he was doing: fighting Libya, only on a much larger scale.

As the television war continued, as the initial exaggerated optimism faded but the President's standing in the polls remained high, indeed at unprecedented levels of approval, those in Congress who voted against him in January returned home to deal with their constituents who were frequently unhappy with how they had voted and sometimes openly and aggressively unforgiving. The President's so-called gamble, which made him appear strong-willed and determined, which would one day show him also to have been prescient, received its most visible manifestation of popular support in the yellow ribbons that sprouted everywhere and in the more conspicuous display of American flags, his symbol, the one he had so strenuously defended and fought for in his election campaign against the much less patriotic Michael Dukakis.

With most of the nation loyally spurring America on, the war continued. The Scud missile that evaded the American-Israeli defenses over Tel Aviv and crashed into a suburb, causing death, devastation, and injury, might have led the Israelis to wish to retaliate against Iraq; instead, it brought them to ask for another $13 billion in aid from the United States—$3 billion to compensate for existing and anticipated war damages, $10 billion, over five years, to assist in the resettlement of Jewish immigrants from the Soviet Union. Israel, despite its reputation for military realism, knew the Bush administration not at all. It is conceivable, of course, that the Prime Minister and his colleagues wrongly estimated the importance in the Bush hierarchy of the Deputy Secretary of State, Lawrence Eagleburger, who had been sent to keep them in order, which translated as refraining from engaging in offensive military operations. They may have interpreted it as a larger pledge of continued moral and other support. If so, the Israelis knew less than they pretended. Eagleburger carried no great weight with the President; only Baker existed for the President, and Baker's fondness for the Jewish state was, to put it generously, muted. In any case, the Israelis wholly misinterpreted the interests of the President. While grateful that Israel had done nothing to ruin his carefully wrought Coalition, Bush was not about to translate that gratitude into a wish to make new appropriations of billions of dollars. Did Israel not know that the United States was poor, very poor?

Regular network television, restored to something like its old news schedules after the first weeks of the war, and CNN, still reporting war news around the clock, took for granted that they were performing a major public service. Indeed, the promise, on the three major American commercial networks, that regular programs would be interrupted for special news bulletins—an air-raid alarm in Tel Aviv, for example—suggested how seriously the war was being taken, how imperative it was that the American public be kept informed, at every moment. Why the public needed to know such things few dared to ask. It would have suggested an attitude of light-heartedness inappropriate to grave and dangerous times. The more distressing question, never posed, was whether the constant television blather was in fact providing the historical and social context of the war, thus imparting to the American people information that they needed to have. Was the country being informed about matters of consequence that would make ordinary citizens understand Iraq and Kuwait better? Were Iran and Israel, Saudi Arabia and Egypt, Syria and Jordan emerging as real places, with specific problems peculiar to each and very different from those of the United States? Did it matter at all if the answer was no?

CNN broadcasts, watched around the world, helped give its stock new value, exceeding by far what even the most intrepid and speculative investor would have imagined possible on August 1. Cable television, as the United States had come to know it, was clearly a growth industry. Some went so far as to say that it would be one of the permanent beneficiaries of the Gulf War. While many in the United States welcomed a service that existed at all hours of the day and night, a convenience of unimaginable importance, many who watched it abroad— and their numbers were legion—noted what they took to be CNN's distinctly American bias. Even those who accepted American values and explanations raised questions not frequently heard in or near CNN's Atlanta headquarters.

When, for example, CNN's Peter Arnett was criticized for his broadcasts out of Baghdad, for allegedly allowing himself to be used by Saddam to propagandize, American journalists and television commentators identified with him and rallied 'round; a man of unrivaled journalistic talent who had first made his name in Vietnam was being crucified by know-nothings. These same men wanted to prevent him from plying his trade, reporting on what a too strict American censorship prevented others from saying and doing. Outside the Fourth Estate, opinions were more divided on whether Peter Arnett was in fact contributing to the war effort. The last was thought to be a citizen's obligation, though the phrase itself was studiously avoided. Since most citizens were doing nothing except watching television, it became difficult to ask: And what did you do during the Gulf War? Still, journalists, in part because of the attacks on Arnett, but also because restrictions on their

movements were so severe, began to ask more insistently
whether they had not in effect been co-opted by the government
and were being used for the Pentagon's purposes. Too few
asked the more fundamental question: Were they not being
used for the *President's* purposes?

Such discussion never surfaced among those who heatedly
debated Arnett's talent, lauded his journalistic skills, recalled
his brilliant reporting years earlier in Vietnam, and wholly
missed the only important story worth telling: television news
was retailing an essentially antiseptic account of the war, with
its heroes and villains, essentially a story of what could be
filmed, of what the censor allowed the camera to see, of what
the White House considered fit for national consumption in
terms of what the President and his Secretary of State had
decided the story would be. And so the Gulf War was represented as a clean war—a contradiction in terms—even on the
Coalition side, where only "smart bombs" were being dropped,
on military targets exclusively, intended to achieve one purpose,
to force the evil dictator to shout quits.

George Bush, like his teacher Ronald Reagan, knew how
useful it was to craft simple arguments, to disseminate them,
and to win public approval through their being believed. The
news conveyed on American television was certainly believed,
though it was in fact invented, having been packaged to
communicate very simple, almost primordial patriotic sentiments. Even the exultation after the Coalition "victory" was
never spontaneous; it was a staged event, like many of the
others that occurred during the war itself. From the war's
beginnings, the White House dominated the airwaves; it was
as if Congress had adjourned after January 16. No one inquired
into what senators were thinking, doing, or saying. All activity
of the kind that serious men and women attended to was
thought to be occurring in and around the White House.
Members of Congress were perhaps responding to their mail,
their constituents, but this was not news. Only the President,

responding to the latest Saddam threat, was newsworthy; he deserved his prime place on television.

On a single day, January 25, *The New York Times* told more about what was going on in the world, and at home, described more provocatively and intelligently the issues dividing societies and communities, not to speak of differences within the United States, than anything CNN and the major networks provided in a week of televised broadcasting. Thus, for example, the *Times* reported from Cairo on a two-hour speech President Mubarak had delivered before a special meeting of the elected Egyptian Parliament that met in joint session with his appointed Consultative Council. Mubarak, seeking to offset a growing internal criticism of the war in which Egypt was participating as an ally of the United States, expressed his affection for the people of Iraq and concern for their welfare. Saying that Saddam's future was not a matter of great interest to him, that the people of Iraq would decide that issue, he proceeded to address the question that clearly preoccupied many in his audience. For those who argued that the Americans were quick to condemn Iraq's aggression against Kuwait but showed no comparable concern with the plight of the Palestinians, Mubarak, in the words of the news report, "strongly implied that Egypt and Saudi Arabia had pledges from President Bush to look into the Palestinian issue once the Gulf crisis is settled." Was this true? Did it mean anything? What, precisely, had the American President promised to do? Or was Mubarak, a leader sorely tried at home, simply feeling the necessity to say something that would relieve him of specific internal political pressures?

His equally important statement, perhaps, was his defense of the decision he had taken to enter the war against Iraq. He insisted that Egypt, in sending troops to Saudi Arabia, acted in accord with "specific contractual obligations, which we view with the utmost seriousness and rigor." For those in the United States who might mistakenly imagine that Mubarak was simply responding to the call of the United Nations, that he was acting in accord with his country's obligations to that body, the *Times* explained his true meaning: the reference was not to UN Security Council resolutions, but to "Egypt's participation in Arab League mutual defense accords." Those were serious and binding engagements for the Egyptian President. He took action not because Saddam Hussein had lied to him—which he had—but because of specific treaty obligations to others, including a rich Arab state whose friendship he coveted. Mubarak wanted to be part of the Arab League; he wanted to prove himself a faithful partner.

His reticences about other matters did nothing to prevent an attack later that day from a spokesman for eight Egyptian opposition parties, himself a senior official of the Progressive Alignment Party, who indicated that a petition would soon be circulated asking for the end of the war, described as "a savage American attack on the Iraqi people." *The New York Times* went on to note that all the opposition parties in Egypt, except for the Wafd Party, strongly opposed the war; if Egyptian troops were to remain in Saudi Arabia, they wished for them to be moved to the western part of the country, so that they might participate in the defense of two holy shrines, at Mecca and Medina. Islamic fundamentalism—a subject much mentioned by all who reflected on the changing scene in the whole of North Africa and the Middle East—scarcely figured in the three-minute television sound bites that told of Egypt's commitment of 45,000 troops to the Coalition. While news was rarely explicitly suppressed on American television, it most often spoke the language Ronald Reagan and George Bush used, which explained why those who governed the medium had such limited concern with instruction and were so totally preoccupied with ratings.

If those whose war news was largely provided by American television knew little of the fissures in the Muslim world, and cared not a whit what Algeria or Pakistan might be thinking or doing, the interest in America's allies in Western Europe was not appreciably greater. While all were technically members of the Coalition, and at least three had contributed military units of some consequence, few in the United States cared about how they were faring, let alone how they viewed the war. Antiwar demonstrations in Germany or elsewhere—visually compelling—figured from time to time, but the idea that the war, in the words of a major headline in *The New York Times*, had "shattered" Europe's fragile unity was rarely admitted, and certainly never explored. The war was having consequences that those who paid attention only to events in the desert as interpreted by the White House could not imagine. Yet discussion of such political issues, employing data gathered from diverse sources and reflecting opinion in the capitals of Europe, was not a feature of the talk shows that made American television a nightly chore.

It is not only television's failure to represent the substance of what was happening abroad that needs to be noted; its reporting on the United States showed the same tendency to dwell on the pictorial, to select the familiar, to make its appeal to sentiment when it might have addressed political and social issues of greater moment. Any number of television programs documented the difficulties women called from the reserves into the services experienced as they sought to make provision for their young children and took leave of their families. These stories, which took a hundred forms, including those that dwelled on all the roles assigned to women in the armed services, evaded the only fundamental one which a visit to an Army installation would have immediately revealed. The armed forces of the United States had become recognizably black. *The New York Times* said it all in noting that while one in eight Americans was black, one in four of those serving in the Gulf was black. The situation that had prevailed at the time of Vietnam had been greatly exacerbated by additional years of inner-city poverty, with high levels of minority unemployment and underemployment. Too many young black men, otherwise destined for menial dead-end jobs, the children of struggling, single-parent families, hoped they could rescue themselves in one of the military services. Some entered out of ambition and others out of economic necessity; no one could know for certain how much the second figured in the decisions of those who were now poised to fight in the Gulf.

In *The New York Times*'s page one story entitled "Blacks Wary of Their Big Role as Troops," reference was made to the "deep well of resentment and anger in some blacks who fear that their community will pay disproportionately for a war that many of them do not support." Statistics, in this instance, did not lie. If casualties proved to be large, blacks would by definition suffer disproportionately. The more interesting detail concerned the fact that many in the black community were said to be opposed to the war. Why should that be? If true, had that information been communicated in the thousands of hours of television broadcasting? CBS, for example, had recently collaborated with *The New York Times* in a poll which indicated that whites supported military action over the continued use of sanctions by a majority of four to one; blacks, in the same poll, were seen to be evenly divided. Had the other television networks given the poll any attention, or did they not wish to advertise the findings of a competitor? In any case, how many knew that all black members of the House of Representatives opposed the use of force and preferred to continue with sanctions? The *Times* also reported that blacks were forming antiwar groups to persuade other blacks not to join the armed forces.

Though the *Times* account told little of the precise incidence of such black sentiment, let alone the size of the groups formed, or whether they were common in certain black communities only, the phenomenon called for some explanation. Did anger with the Bush administration, for its failure to offer any substantial help to blacks, to make any practical efforts at resolving the problems of crime and drugs that plagued the inner cities, explain the reported disenchantment with the war? Perhaps. Was the opposition principally an expression of dismay with the government's reputed insensitivity more generally to minority group demands? Possibly. Still, the story documented the pride some blacks felt in the fact that the Chairman of the Joint Chiefs of Staff was a black man; others expressed their total agreement with the President that, given Iraq's aggression and the threat it posed to the Middle East, the United States had no choice but to act in the way it did. If an Assistant Secretary of Defense, rather incautiously, pointed out that no one had forced black men and women to enlist, he intended the remark only as a compliment: "They're not victims, they're willing patriotic Americans." What higher accolade could the Pentagon give its black service personnel?

Was it inevitable that a son of the Reverend Martin Luther King, Jr., would urge black soldiers not to fight? His words were as precise as those General Powell habitually used; he said: "Every black soldier ought to say: 'You all do what you want to. I'm not going to fight. This is not my war.' " If blacks joined the armed forces principally to escape their poverty, as many insisted was the case, should they now risk their lives for that society? They were recruited with promises of education and training; they had entered one of the few relatively integrated institutions in American society, where they could expect to rise, and even exercise a certain authority over whites. They had not bargained for war. Why should they suffer it? Would this not be one more instance where blacks would be decimated, while whites, less talented and less educated, who entered the services not out of necessity but for other reasons, never explained, would be preserved? The debate was acrimonious. It returned always to the theme that the Reverend Jesse Jackson focused on: the blacks were in the Gulf in such great number because they had nowhere else to go; the bleakness of their economic opportunities made the war their unintended destiny.

There was no place for such candor, or indeed such confu-

sion, on American television. Saddam Hussein soon provided
it with an event that brought millions back to their television
screens. The millions of gallons of crude oil deliberately
released by the Iraqis from a Kuwaiti offshore terminal threatened to do vast environmental damage in the Gulf, comparable
certainly to what had been produced by the accidental discharge
of oil by the *Exxon Valdez* disaster in 1989. American and world
television became transfixed by the threat to wildlife and fishing,
to desalinization plants in Saudi Arabia, and, for Americans,
by the potential risk to the amphibious military landings said
to be in an advanced state of preparation. The possibility that
the Iraqis would set fire to the oil, threatening allied warships
in the region, was not excluded. The President called it a "sick"
act of a desperate man; his contempt for Saddam grew with
each of his television appearances.

The oil spill remained television's principal spectacle; with
it, however, soon came a new concern, which could not be
pictorially rendered. Why were Iraqi planes taking off for Iran?
Were they being flown by airmen deserting their embattled
leader in Baghdad? Or was it another of Saddam's sinister
plots, and if so, what did it signify? The war had reached a
point where everyone was guessing how the major actors would
play their remaining cards. It was easier for old Washington
hands to reflect about the President's plans than to guess what
the man in his bunker in Baghdad was thinking.

On January 29, when the President came to the Capitol for
his triumphal State of the Union speech, applause resounded
throughout the chamber and across the airwaves for a man
who promised that the "indomitable" American character
would overcome all difficulties, both at home and abroad. Using
his conventional World War II images, the President intoned:
"Together, we have resisted the trap of appeasement, cynicism
and isolation that gives temptation to tyrants." A nation that
had "done the hard work of freedom" was prepared to "lead
the world in facing down a threat to decency and humanity."

Warming to his theme, he continued: "What is at stake is more than one small country, it is a big idea—a new world order where diverse nations are drawn together in common cause to achieve the universal aspirations of mankind: peace and security, freedom and the rule of law. Such a world is worthy of our struggle, and worthy of our children's future."

Answering the irritating critics who might be questioning his policies in the Baltic republics, the President said: "The end of the Cold War has been a victory for all humanity. . . . Europe has become whole and free, and America's leadership was instrumental in making it possible." Turning specifically to the Soviet Union and the Baltic states, he said: "Our relationship to the Soviet Union is important, not only to us but to the world. That relationship has helped to shape these and other historic changes. But, like many other nations, we have been deeply concerned by the violence in the Baltics, and we have communicated that concern to the Soviet leadership."

What had he done to express this concern? The President said: "The principle that has guided us is simple: our objective is to help the Baltic peoples achieve their aspirations, not to punish the Soviet Union. In our recent discussions with the Soviet leadership we have been given representations which, if fulfilled, would result in the withdrawal of some Soviet forces, a reopening of dialogue with the republics, and a move away from violence." He promised to "watch carefully as the situation develops." And to express the full extent of his confidence in the Soviet leadership, he added: "And we will maintain our contact with the Soviet leadership to encourage continued commitment to democratization and reform." Would anyone listening to these words know how much had changed in the Soviet Union, and not only in the Baltic republics? Would anyone guess that *perestroika* was dead and *glasnost* embattled? For the President, who wished only "a more peaceful future for all mankind," continued United States-Soviet cooperation was imperative, "if it is possible."

The President, for much of his speech, spoke in the glittering ambiguities characteristic of his inaugural address. Still, the speech was interrupted more than forty times by applause, including accolades for the wives of General Powell and General Schwarzkopf, each of whom he took care to introduce. It was a superbly staged performance, ideally suited to television. Avoiding any specific reference to the terms of the peace that would follow on Iraq's expulsion from Kuwait, or even what his increasingly shopworn phrase, the "new world order," implied, the speech was intentionally inspirational, suited to a day when patriotism was the political coin of the realm.

Television convention allowed the Democrats to reply, though without, of course, the benefit of an inspired live audience. Senator George Mitchell, the Majority Leader, took his obligation seriously. His speech, in contrast to that of the President, was flat and prosaic, apologetic where it need not have been, trying to explain once again the Democratic Party's position in the debates in Congress on the use of force before the fighting had actually begun. In the only foreign policy reference that had any originality, Mitchell reminded his viewers that "the dictator we help today may turn his weapons on us tomorrow." Mitchell, recalling that "for ten years, U.S. policy favored Iraq," urged that such a serious mistake not be repeated. The rest of the speech largely addressed domestic issues, which the President had carefully skirted. There was no contest on the television tube that night. The President knew precisely how to use the medium; the senator from Maine mistook the occasion for a seminar.

As the war ground on into February, the Germans agreed to allocate $5.5 billion more, to show their solidarity with the United States, but also to blunt growing criticism abroad. The Israelis were said to be losing patience with the slowness of the war. If only their air force would be let loose, many suggested, all would be rapidly ended. One television commentator, speaking with Defense Minister Moshe Arens, voiced a sentiment common in the country: "The Americans keep bombing launchers, but haven't been terribly effective. Meanwhile, Americans are watching the Super Bowl, and Israelis are sitting in shelters and sealed rooms." To which the Defense Minister replied: "The situation you described isn't going to continue —not two months, and not a month. I simply estimate that a situation in which we'll be neutral or not active, and their ability to launch missiles against us isn't eliminated, it won't continue for a long time." The Israelis were yearning to be taken off their leash; only the Americans were preventing them from taking action, ending the threat to their cities. All this was being said while Turkish fundamentalists argued that Turkey ought to leave the Coalition entirely; the war should be settled by Muslims, not by outsiders. These were not the words the American television public heard; instead, they listened to tales of new and even greater American victories in the skies over Kuwait and Iraq.

Again, it was the press that provided the counterpoint for these skimpy and one-sided television accounts. William Safire, writing in *The New York Times*, described a situation where American airmen were winning and American diplomats were losing. If Safire's sources could be credited, the Secretary of State in his recent Washington conversations had made unfortunate concessions to the new Soviet Foreign Minister, Aleksandr Bessmertnykh. It appeared that both continued to believe that a cessation of hostilities was possible if Iraq made an unequivocal commitment to leave Kuwait. Safire found the words "continue to" offensive, but took issue also with the idea that a "commitment" from Iraq would be sufficient. In his mind, the more grievous error was to suggest that if the Iraqis did agree to go, there would be discussions of the "causes of instability in the region," together with a study of the "sources of conflict." The Soviet Foreign Minister, in Safire's view, had secured an agreement from the Secretary of State that invited "the Butcher of Baghdad to turn certain defeat into a kind of

victory." Though the President's press secretary suggested that
their joint statement had been misinterpreted and that there
had been no change in policy, Safire had his doubts, particularly
when the President said that he had "no differences" with his
Secretary of State.

The anger of Safire, rarely communicated with quite the
same force even by those few who habitually shouted and
ranted on television—Bush and his close associates studiously
avoided doing that—was contained in two short paragraphs
that contained the following words: "Let's not kid ourselves;
our goal is not only to remove Saddam from Kuwait but to
remove Saddam from power—period. No comebacks with
stashed away aircraft or hidden nuclear potential." To emphasize his position even more strongly, he continued: "If diplomatic niceties, superpower relations or the sensitivities of the
Coalition prevent us from blurting out this truth, the least our
Secretary of State can do is bite his tongue and refrain from
frittering away the goal our forces are fighting to win." This
was press talk, not television talk, at least not conventional
television talk, which generally maintained the proprieties, and
would not even say that the President had delivered himself
of a message so ambiguous and so pusillanimous as to insult
the intelligence of the nation. No one said it, perhaps, because
no one believed it.

The war was going well, at least in the skies. All else was
secondary. Few body bags were returning home; the fears of
the Cassandras had proved unfounded. When, on February 3,
the front page of *The New York Times* carried a story on four
years of Gorbachev, from hope to disillusion, it spoke of a
thaw that had become a chill. The reporter, Bill Keller, writing
from Moscow, told a tale familiar to those who had been
observing the Soviet scene, but largely irrelevant to those who
had been listening only to the President or to television since
the start of the war. Keller told the story that "Z" (Martin
Malia) had told a year before, when most of its readers cared

only to discover Z's identity. By early 1991, what much of the world refused to believe in 1990 had come to pass. The Soviet economic experiments had not worked; the cultural thaw, so grandiloquently and imaginatively promised with *glasnost*, had turned to ice and frozen; the Communist Party was moribund, but Soviet society had not become democratic.

Only in the West, and particularly in Washington, was there still an expectation that telephonic conversation with the Soviet leader—perhaps additional summits or, in their absence, meetings of the two "superpower" Foreign Ministers—would make the Kremlin see the light of day. If events in the Baltic republics were discouraging, and many in Congress worried about what might be impending, the White House and the State Department concluded that unreasonable men like Boris Yeltsin took insufficient account of Gorbachev's problems and failed to understand the need for patience. They remembered that Gorbachev removed Soviet troops from Afghanistan, negotiated major arms control agreements, reduced arsenals and armies in Europe, and in effect repudiated the Brezhnev doctrine, allowing the Eastern European regimes to move away from Soviet control; these things alone made him a unique Soviet figure, worthy of commendation. The growing tide of protest and disillusion in the Soviet Union was ignored by the networks, its magnitude relegated to the print press. The mass media story was still the war.

But the war now refused to cooperate. The news had taken on a certain sameness day after day, and there were few new arresting pictures, certainly none to compare with American airmen taken prisoner, criticizing the war, or birds destroyed by a massive oil spill—and there was, inevitably, some movement away from the television screen. People were again reported to be going off on vacation. They did not travel abroad, which was still thought to be much too dangerous— London and Frankfurt, for example, were off-limits even for businessmen who understood the hazards of Arab terrorism—

but California, Florida, and all manner of other American resorts beckoned. Life was returning to normal in the United States. The show went on, but without its earlier interest. CNN lost something of its following.

If the President of Iran indicated a wish to negotiate a settlement between the United States and Iraq, it received a quick rejection from the State Department. "What's to mediate?" Margaret Tutwiler said. "We would be pleased, obviously, if anyone could get Saddam Hussein to comply with these UN resolutions. The only mediation in our opinion that would be appropriate would be for the people who communicate with Saddam Hussein to convince him to comply with the twelve UN resolutions." It was just as simple as that—news for a three-minute sound bite—but not news to provoke any major discussion of what Rafsanjani had in mind, or why he had sought to insert himself at that point. A Soviet effort of the same kind might have been less brusquely rejected, but then the Soviet Union was not Iran. Enfeebled as it might be, it was still a state to be reckoned with.

By the end of the first week of February, a new message came across the airwaves. The President, expressing skepticism that air strikes alone would suffice to force Saddam out of Kuwait, opened a debate which allowed the Pentagon increasingly to acknowledge that while the bombs had done great damage to Iraq, they had not seriously weakened the Republican Guards, Iraq's elite troops. While the President refrained from saying that a ground war would be necessary, his sending the Defense Secretary and the Chairman of the Joint Chiefs of Staff to confer with the commander in the field, General Schwarzkopf, suggested that such an operation would be considered. In his usual manner, the President indicated that the decision would be difficult but he was prepared to make it. Always courageous, and never disinclined to say so, but also commendably courteous to his subordinates, at least in public, he added that he knew that the decision would not be recommended to him "unless these people I just mentioned know that it's the right thing to do." The nation waited for the advertised meeting, and the talk shows began to discuss the pros and cons of a ground offensive.

In *The New York Times*, other subjects figured. Page one stories told of the Soviets increasing their army patrols, extending their crackdown to eighty-six cities, but also of growing concern by Americans that the Soviet ardor for new arms control agreements was waning. It appeared that the military influence in Moscow was reasserting itself, and that this was having an effect on Gorbachev's ability to pursue his objectives. The *Times*, in its sober reporting, noted that the increased unhappiness in the Soviet military with the reduction in the size of Soviet conventional forces in Europe had made the most recent visit of the Soviet Foreign Minister to Washington a disappointing one. Meanwhile, in Moscow, the attacks on "economic and street crime" continued; opposition groups worried that all this was camouflage, a prelude to even tougher Kremlin measures.

With ample camera crews in Moscow, the networks might have done more to emphasize the words of Yuri Afanasyev, a leading opposition figure, who repeated in February what Shevardnadze had said in December: "A very obvious turn to the right has occurred and we are moving toward the restoration of totalitarianism." But such news clearly could not compare with the more important matter of whether or not there would be an American ground offensive in the Gulf sometime soon.

The bombings outside Number 10 Downing Street diverted the television cameras for a day, though only long enough to establish that this was not the work of Arab terrorists but only of the IRA, that relatively uninteresting band of early-twentieth-century freedom fighters who continued to plague the United Kingdom, finding some support also among Irish-Americans but having no importance for the world outside. In short, such stories were local events essentially, though the idea that the whole of the British Cabinet might have been destroyed did provide a vulgar thrill in some quarters.

As the television pundits debated whether or not a ground offensive would be necessary, and whether it ought to take place sooner or later, and all waited the return of Cheney and Powell, the two principals who would tell the President what to do—the final hard decision being his, of course—the Sunday talk shows found room for the other key players. Secretary of State Baker, at home in Washington for a few days, appeared on *Face the Nation*, one of the three great network Sunday television entertainments. The words of President Gorbachev, delivered just a day previously, suggesting that the United States air strikes were taking on "an ever more alarming and dramatic scope," that there was reason to be worried over whether the United Nations mandate was not being exceeded, brought a courteous but candid reply from the secretary. Baker explained: "The language calls for the use of all necessary means to implement the UN resolutions, which call for Iraq's immediate and unconditional withdrawal from Kuwait and restoration of the leadership. So, by taking on targets in Iraq, we are moving in that direction, and we're doing so in a manner that's going to reduce Coalition casualties."

Asked whether he feared that Gorbachev might be signaling a shift in Soviet policy, a drift away from his earlier acceptance of the need for an anti-Iraq coalition, Baker expressed his complete confidence that this was not happening. In his view, the Soviet President was simply seeking to placate internal Soviet constituencies. Indeed, to suggest how intimate United States-Soviet relations were, the secretary added: "The Soviet Union gave us prior notice of this statement." Could amity take a more concrete form? Why, then, had Gorbachev spoken in the way he did? Baker explained: "It is true that the position, the principled position they have taken alongside the United States, has not been popular with many segments of Soviet society. So there is a significant amount of public opinion in the Soviet Union, particularly in the Muslim republics, with some of the military, that they're very much opposed to the position they're taking, but they're sticking with that position." American intelligence on "public opinion" in the Muslim republics was either very extraordinary or Gorbachev was telling his friends even more than some imagined possible. In either case, no one thought to ask the secretary whether "public opinion," in the form he described, existed in the Soviet Union and how it managed to express itself.

On the rival *Meet the Press* program, Senator Robert Dole showed a somewhat more cautious respect for the Gorbachev position, while remaining steadfast, of course, in support of the Bush administration. Like the Soviet President, he worried that the Americans, in meting out their military punishment, might be going beyond the strict limits settled on by the United Nations. Still, he expressed confidence that this was not the President's explicit intention. It was "happenstance" that, in trying to move the Iraqis out of Kuwait, the Americans were compelled to move against targets in Iraq. The Minority Leader of the Senate could see nothing wrong with that. How else could the Iraqis be dislodged? Republicans spoke with a single voice on that Sunday, as they did on every previous occasion in parroting the wisdom of the President's strategy, and there were no Democrats about to ask whether the time had not come to consider what the United States proposed to do when Saddam was defeated. To do that, openly, was to challenge the President in his political objective, to make the war seem an exceedingly difficult and hazardous venture, where victory was the sole objective, and peace could take only a single form.

When, several days later, Saddam, meeting with Yevgeny Primakov, Gorbachev's personal emissary, announced on Iraqi radio that he would be willing to cooperate with the Soviet Union in finding a way to end the war, he gave concrete evidence of his weakness. The fact that he joined the statement to one expressing his determination to keep fighting "until aggression and the aggressors are beaten back" gave the administration the freedom to disparage both remarks. Marlin Fitzwater, the White House spokesman, noted that Saddam had said nothing about leaving Kuwait. That was the bottom line, and until some specific actions were taken to conform with the United Nations resolutions, nothing had changed.

It appeared that Saddam had said more than was reported on American television. While he explicitly linked the Gulf War to larger regional problems, making specific reference to Palestine, he spoke also of the Allied intention to destroy Iraq, to obliterate its civilian infrastructure. This was all part of the imperialist-Zionist conspiracy to dominate the region. This segment of the broadcast, obviously addressed to the Iraqi people and the Arab world more generally, was almost secondary to another message, specifically intended for one man, the Soviet President, Mikhail Gorbachev. In desperation, Saddam spoke of the Soviet Union having "a legal, political and moral responsibility" to act, to help Iraq. His words were carefully chosen: "The differing Iraqi and Soviet perspectives on the Gulf situation do not justify condoning the crimes committed by the United States under the cover of Resolution 678, or allowing them to continue. What is required now is for resolute action to stop these savage crimes and to keep the United States from using the United Nations as a vehicle for attaining its imperialist objectives."

The man so feared in the West—the "butcher of Baghdad" —still imagined that the Soviets were in a position to help him. He ought to have known better; his reputed craftiness and love of power ought to have told him that there was nothing Gorbachev could threaten Bush with, that he could not even persuade him to come to a negotiating table. Whatever Gorbachev's motives might be for wishing to intrude, however much he might imagine the Soviet Union stood to gain by being the "peacemaker," he lacked the resources to do so. The

President of the United States knew this; more importantly, his plan required a total victory, and neither the Soviet Union nor Iraq would be allowed to deny him that prize.

When, a day later, two bombs dropped in Baghdad by American Stealth bombers destroyed a concrete building in a residential neighborhood, killing hundreds of civilians, television was given a new "spectacular." As reports trickled in of protests in many Arab nations, of revulsion with what the Americans were doing to destroy Baghdad, there was a new sense of the fragility of the Coalition so arduously cobbled together. The worries, again, were exaggerated. Within a day of the bombing—an incident that a strong Iraq would have exploited for weeks—the Iraqis announced their readiness to comply with the United Nations resolutions. A statement read over Baghdad radio, in the name of the Revolutionary Command Council, brought jubilant gunfire in Baghdad and expressions of relief and joy in many parts of the world. The President, not entirely alone among those who questioned whether the event merited celebration, warned that it might all be a "cruel hoax." The moment's euphoria faded within hours of its sudden appearance.

The Soviet Union, however, did not doubt the authenticity of the offer. Moscow, in welcoming the announcement, told of an earlier message sent to the United States, Great Britain, and France, asking that no ground offensive be started until discussions scheduled for the following week between the Soviet President and the Iraqi Foreign Minister had occurred. Again, the Soviets were seeking to be "peacemakers." From many quarters now, the plea arose that a ground war, with the terrible destruction it promised, had to be avoided.

That the President had no interest in convincing Saddam Hussein to surrender, that instead he desperately craved a victory that would ensure his own reelection, was what no one cared to acknowledge. The war, in the President's mind, was intended to be a final judgment on his own remarkable political and diplomatic abilities, the almost equally marvelous talents of his Secretary of State, and the return to respectability and self-esteem of a military still said to be demoralized by the sapped confidence of its Vietnam experience. The war was also intended to say more, though much less openly: the President was announcing the demise of the strong Soviet Union of the Cold War. Without his being insulting—and there was no reason for him to be that—he would display the Soviet Union as a "paper tiger," able to flex its muscles but unable to change anything. The Soviet military could be expected to understand what the remarkable display of American military power demonstrated about the unique qualities of the American democracy. The President's political scenario—for it was only that—wildly exaggerated American power, equated military strength with other, more intangible things, very much in the way the country did when it first developed its atomic capability; it took no account of America's severe economic and social distress, which prevented it from acting in the world in the way it once imagined it might do.

But here the President's innocence revealed itself unmistakably. While he knew precisely what he was doing when he chose to go to war, he had no idea of how to make peace—not so much with Iraq, a relatively inconsequential pawn in the larger international arena—but with all the others who doubted him even as they indulged him. Yet for any commentator to have said this would have been inconceivable. It would have suggested that victory in Iraq did not create the conditions for peace in the Middle East. The dissolution of the Soviet empire—however welcome—did not create conditions that would allow for a reassertion of American hegemony.

In the days that followed, the full extent of Soviet weakness was revealed, for those who cared to look. As the Kremlin gained new information on what Saddam was prepared to accept, as it realized the full extent of his obduracy, the earlier enthusiasm for his offer faded. When Gorbachev met with Iraq's Foreign Minister, Tariq Aziz, the Soviet President presented his own formula for an immediate cease-fire. Reports emanating from Moscow suggested that he urged an immediate and total withdrawal from Kuwait, agreeing to protect Iraq's sovereignty, to summon a Middle East peace conference. Gorbachev's spokesman called it a plea that "reflected the principled position of the U.S.S.R." In Washington, Bush's spokesman said: "Our military campaign remains on schedule." Would Aziz, hurrying back to Baghdad, bring the good word in time, telling the world what it most wanted to hear, that Saddam had accepted Gorbachev's offer?

Hopes did not remain high for very long. The President, without divulging the terms of the Soviet offer, and going out of his way not to reject it, said that it "falls well short of what would be required" for the war to be halted. America's two most faithful allies in Europe, Great Britain and France, joined in casting doubt on whether the Gorbachev terms went far enough in satisfying the United Nations demands. American officials were said to be under strict orders not to discuss the Gorbachev proposals. On Capitol Hill, according to *The New York Times*, the Secretary of Defense, appearing before a congressional committee, unnamed, said that "it would be a mistake to pause for negotiations."

When, a day later, press reports indicated that both the United States and Great Britain, in separate statements, had informed Moscow that its terms were unacceptable, because they provided no very "tight timetable" for Iraq's withdrawal from Kuwait, but also because they did not make sufficiently explicit Iraq's obligations to accept all twelve United Nations resolutions, it was clear that even Saddam's acceptance would not bring the war to an immediate end. The ball lay again in the Soviet court, and there was one last chance to play it. On February 22, at 2:40 a.m., a spokesman for Gorbachev announced in Moscow that Iraq had given a "positive" response to a new seven-point Soviet peace proposal, which omitted any mention of a Middle East peace conference.

The terms were simple enough: Iraq agreed to a full and

unconditional withdrawal from Kuwait; the withdrawal would begin on the second day after the fighting stopped; it would be completed in a fixed period, not specifically stated; United Nations economic sanctions would lapse when Iraq had taken two-thirds of its forces out of Kuwait; all other resolutions against Iraq would end just as soon as all Iraqi forces left Kuwait; all prisoners of war would be released immediately after the cease-fire; the United Nations Security Council would designate countries not involved in the conflict to oversee the Iraqi withdrawal.

The White House response was explicit. Marlin Fitzwater explained that the President had received a telephone call from his Soviet counterpart and had spoken with him for thirty-three minutes, thanking him for his "intensive and useful efforts," but raising "serious concerns about several points in the plan." In the questioning that followed, it emerged that the President proposed to consult his allies, that it was too early to give a definitive response. When asked specifically whether the Soviet President was not negotiating in America's behalf, Fitzwater responded emphatically: "We haven't asked him [Gorbachev] to do anything. He's asked our views on these matters. We'll provide them as we have in the last few days. But I reiterate again that this is a matter between the Soviets and Iraq, and we are appreciative of the communication that has told us of these discussions but we are not a part of the negotiations."

The proprieties had been observed. No deliberate effort had been made to humiliate the Soviet President. When, however, President Bush indicated in the Rose Garden that Iraq must begin to withdraw its forces from Kuwait by Saturday, notifying the United Nations to that effect and completing the withdrawal in seven days, it was obvious that both Iraq and the Soviet Union had lost. The smoking oil wells of Kuwait gave the latest pictorial expression of Iraqi barbarism. The next news reported that Saddam had ignored Bush's ultimatum and the start of the ground campaign. For the first time in months, the President was open with the American people; he promised a swift and decisive victory. Four days later, Bush halted the fighting; the vaunted Republican Guards had been vanquished; Kuwait had been liberated; Iraq had been humbled. The United States had kept its pledge to the United Nations.

The Six-Week War was over, not with a bang, and certainly not with a whimper. Extravagant praise was lavished on all who had achieved such remarkable things. Months later, it was still possible for informed men in Washington to speak of the war as "a defining moment in military history, a campaign as momentous in operational terms as Cannae, Agincourt, Waterloo, the Somme, or Normandy." One could hear the gales of laughter bursting from departed heroes—Churchill, de Gaulle, and Eisenhower. The unique achievement of the Gulf war was neither the rapid deployment of large forces nor the use of new and advanced military technologies—on both counts, World War II compared very favorably—but the enlistment of mass public support through the expert manipulation of one twentieth-century communications medium, television. The war began with aerial photographs of the bombing of Baghdad; it ended with a black American soldier reassuring an Iraqi prisoner of war that he was safe; all was well. The war was a tale manufactured for television from beginning to end. The story was one worthy of the Gipper himself.

# The New
# World Order

On March 6, 1991, in the House of Representatives, fes-
tooned in red, white, blue, and yellow, the President of
the United States went to receive the homage of a United States
Congress grateful for what he had done to make the Gulf War
short, cheap, and glorious. Those who had doubted him, and
argued for "giving sanctions a chance," dared not absent
themselves from the chamber or withhold their cheers; to do
so would have been churlish, to show an unbecoming lack of
sportsmanship. The President had proved himself right, and
all were expected to acknowledge that, joining in the celebration
of brave American fighting men and women, faithful allies,
able and dedicated military and civilian leaders, all mobilized
and led by the man who stood before them. In a scene more
reminiscent of a political party convention than of the two
houses of Congress assembled in solemn and grateful conclave,
the President thanked one and all for what they had done, and
then proceeded to deliver one of his inspirational messages, of
the kind he learned to give from watching President Reagan.

In his capacity as Commander in Chief, the President told
Congress that "our armed forces fought with honor and valor";

as President, he told the nation that "aggression is defeated. The war is over." The chamber thundered with applause as the President honored both the Coalition and the United Nations. It was, he said, "a victory for unprecedented international cooperation and diplomacy, so well led by our Secretary of State, James Baker. It is a victory for the rule of law and for what is right." He then proceeded to thank Secretary Cheney and General Powell, and then "the tower of calm at the eye of Desert Storm—General Norman Schwarzkopf." Saudi General Khalid, Britain's General de la Billiere, and France's General Roquejoffra were all cited. No specific mention was made of the military forces committed by Italy or Egypt; the necessity of naming Syria as well might have prompted this particular reticence.

The President came, he said, to "speak about the world—the world after war." There had been a villain and a victim; Saddam Hussein and Kuwait. The "darker side of human nature" had been defeated, and the world had to "forge a future" in which it would never again allow itself to be held hostage by such a malign force. The President grieved for all the victims of the war, in Kuwait and elsewhere, but also for the people of Iraq, who "have never been our enemy." He hoped that one day they might again be welcomed into the community of nations.

His compliments to the victors having been paid, he moved on to what he called four key challenges. First, common security arrangements in the region would have to be worked out; friends and allies in the Middle East would be expected to take principal responsibility for these. While the United States had no plan to station ground forces on the Arabian Peninsula, joint air and ground exercises would be undertaken from time to time. The United States Navy, in the region for over forty years, would of course remain there. "Our vital national interests," the President said, "depend on a stable and secure Gulf."

He spoke also of the need to "control the proliferation of weapons of mass destruction and the missiles used to deliver them." A new arms race had to be avoided, and Iraq required "special vigilance." Until its leaders proved conclusively that they would not use their oil revenues to "rearm and rebuild its menacing war machine," Iraq had to be denied "access to the instruments of war."

The President expressed the hope that Israel and the Arab states, so recently obliged to fight a common enemy, would make renewed efforts to resolve their differences, coming together, accepting the need for compromise, all in the cause of peace. The tactics of terrorism led nowhere; they could never be a substitute for diplomacy, he said. The peace had to be grounded in United Nations Security Council Resolutions 242 and 338, which accepted "the principle of territory for peace," the President repeated; he hoped that these would "provide for Israel's security and recognition, and at the same time for legitimate Palestinian political rights." The ending of the Arab-Israeli conflict was imperative; so, also, was the search for solutions to the problem in Lebanon. Finally, the President spoke of the need to foster economic development in the area; the region, "rich in natural resources with a wealth of human potential," had squandered too much on military might for too long; "economic freedom and prosperity for all people of the region" was the imperative need.

Was this, then, what the President meant when he spoke, as he frequently did, of a New World Order? Seeing "a new world coming into view," he quoted his favorite World War II author. The President said: "In the words of Winston Churchill, a 'world order' in which 'the principles of justice and fair play . . . protect the weak against the strong . . .'" The President, elaborating on his own, went on to describe the new world that was coming into view, just beyond the horizon: "A world where the United Nations, freed from Cold War stalemate, is poised to fulfill the historic mission of its founders. A world in which freedom and respect for human rights find a home among all nations." The Gulf War, in the President's words, "put this new world to its first test." He went on to say: "And my fellow Americans: we passed that test." If the New World Order could not "guarantee an era of perpetual peace"—the Iraq war had not been waged as "a war to end all wars"—then "enduring peace must be our mission."

The President of the United States, on an occasion so happy that it lost all pretense to being solemn, failed to describe the world that he saw as coming into being, that all longed to see. His failure could not be attributed only to the insufficiencies of an untalented White House stable of ghostwriters. The unreadiness to portray his vaunted New World Order, to explain how it would happen, what its likely configurations would be, showed the President's ultimate subservience to his teacher, a man equally able to conceal his innocence, creating myths with such daring that he could only be thought simple or shrewd. The President's speech might have been written for President Reagan.

If the President could be believed, the United States had been "transformed" by its victory over Iraq. The brave deeds of American men and women—their confidence and pride— told all Americans what the nation's values were. Responding to what he perceived to be the country's insatiable appetite for self-adulation, he spoke of all that had been proved in the desert, what the brave men and women, responding to the call of duty, "taught us, about our values, about ourselves." Then, in three sentences which in another forum, delivered by another man, in a less elevated position, would have drawn gales of laughter, the President, in his best Reagan manner, said: "We hear so often about our young people in turmoil; how our children fall short; how our schools fail us; how American products and American workers are second-class. Well, don't you believe it. The America we saw in Desert Storm was first-class talent."

A President capable of saying this, knowing the truth, could believe anything. In the wild applause that followed the telling of this pathetic lie about the strength of America's educational and industrial institutions, members of Congress showed more than their fidelity to brave men and women. Confirming what eight years of Reagan and two years of Bush had done to the United States, the corruption of truth that it encouraged and rewarded, the audience lost itself in the President's rhetoric. Could one really question his enthusiasm for America's "state-of-the-art technology," represented by the Patriot missile, or the quality of "the patriots who made it work"? Could one question a man who spoke so feelingly about "soldiers who know about honor and bravery and duty and country and the world-shaking power of these simple words"? Republicans applauded because their man, the victor, was on the podium; Democrats applauded because television cameras were in the room, and any other gesture would have been politically dangerous.

No one, in the days that followed, commented on the banality of the speech. No one said the obvious: that what the President imagined would resolve America's problems was exhortation. In the naïveté of his proposals, but even more in the contempt they showed for the American people, he revealed the true damage done the nation by eight years of Reagan's moralizing. Moreover, the President knew its political effectiveness only too well, and practiced it on every occasion himself. This was the least of his offenses; the more serious one, for the country and the world, was that his New World Order had no content. Again, he showed the attributes he had learned in his terms as Vice President. Why take Congress into his confidence, let alone the nation, particularly when his program lacked substance, and therefore would require no financial appropriations? Again, the President was going to exercise leadership on the cheap, using rhetoric and committing himself to nothing that would require sacrifice from anyone.

It was impossible for him to say that the federal treasury was "bankrupt"—or even to use a more felicitous term, if his White House speechwriters were able to discover one—for to say that was to speak of the damage he and his predecessor had inflicted on the nation. Just as he could not tell the story of the Middle East with any accuracy, since it would only emphasize the failings of successive Republican administrations till August 2, 1990, so he could not say how bankrupt, intellectually and politically, he and his Secretary of State were in thinking about the new world that was forming and that he spoke of so airily. His administration lacked a policy not only for the Middle East but also for the Soviet Union and Eastern Europe, for China and Japan, for India and Pakistan, for the European Community, Africa, and Latin America. While he spoke about the "Cold War" being over, he had no perspective to present about the matter, and no view about what the collapse of Soviet Communism might allow the United States to do. And it was not lack of candor alone that prevented him from telling certain basic truths; it was lack of intellectual capacity, as well as the refusal to abandon or amend the foolproof political strategies he had learned from Ronald Reagan. They had worked admirably for his predecessor; they were working for him; they would work in 1992, which was at the forefront of the President's plan.

In these circumstances, it was easy for him to say what the Secretary of State would do to make peace in the Middle East, to bring the Israelis and the Arabs to a conference table, to assert America's great influence in the region—to complete the process begun by Henry Kissinger, continued by Jimmy Carter, and pursued also by George Shultz in the last months of the Reagan administration. The President, finding no reason to mention any of these earlier negotiations—having no wish to suggest that his policies, such as they were, owed anything to them—showed the contempt that his Secretary of State habitually showed for his immediate predecessor and former

Cabinet colleague, George Shultz. There was no need for the
Secretary to consult Shultz; he had nothing to learn from him.
In any case, Shultz had failed in his efforts with Shamir, and
that alone compromised his standing. Baker intended to succeed, knowing that the Soviet Union would help him in the
matter. He would apply pressure on Israel in a way that no
one else had, and that, he expected, would accomplish his
purpose.

The secretary vastly exaggerated his powers; so, too, did the
President. Both, however, failed in a more important matter;
neither recognized the opportunities created by the failures of
Gorbachev, and neither perceived the new dangers that existed
in the world. Each was a provincial, playing in a world he
scarcely knew.

The homage the President paid to the United Nations and
to human rights seemed strange coming out of the mouth of
a President who had done so little to concern himself with
either over so many years; still, conversions were always possible, and the Democrats could not fail to be pleased to imagine
one in the making. Yet both Republicans and Democrats waited
in vain for the President to be specific. If the Soviet threat had
been lifted, if Saddam had been humbled, where were the new
threats? Why would the U.S. Navy be required to remain in
the Gulf? To do what; to serve where? Why were joint exercises
with Saudi Arabia contemplated? What would they accomplish?
The President spoke in shorthand; the Congress was expected
to understand. In fact, the nation's entire Middle Eastern Gulf
policy, which went back to the days of Dwight Eisenhower, had
always presumed a Soviet or Communist menace. If these no
longer existed, where, then, were the dangers? Did they come
principally from Iran? From Islamic fundamentalism? In any
case, why could the United States so substantially reduce its
military commitments in Central Europe, because of the events
of 1989 and 1990, and not do the same in the Gulf?

To have posed that question would have required Congress

to ask a more fundamental one: how secure did the United States believe Gorbachev's regime to be? If he were to leave, either voluntarily or through a Kremlin "palace revolt," what might the next government look like? How would it comport itself in the Middle East, or in Europe, for that matter? Were these matters of concern to the Bush administration? If so, did they explain the curious reference the President made to not being able to guarantee an "era of perpetual peace," but being concerned only with "enduring peace"? What did *that* ambiguous phrase mean? Had the Gulf War in fact completely transformed the situation in the Middle East? Or was that an illusion? Did Israel see the threat to its security as the United States saw it? What pressures could be generated to make it comply with American wishes? Or did Prime Minister Shamir know what the American President seemed not to understand—that procrastination was itself a negotiating tactic, far more valuable than any provided by the flat rejection of American proposals?

The President spoke airily of acting to control "the proliferation of weapons of mass destruction and the missiles used to deliver them." Was he saying that the United States intended to go out of the arms export business? Would it suddenly deny itself export opportunities in a field scarcely less profitable for it in dollar terms than even that of agricultural exports, and necessary to conceal the extent of the U.S. trade deficit? And if it did so, how would it choose to define arms? Would it stop exporting specific weapons, or would it also seek to control the export of communications systems and other engineering products useful in the development of arms? And if by some extraordinary act of self-denial it did all these things, would it expect others to follow suit? Or did the President intend to summon a World Disarmament Conference, to which he would invite the Soviet Union, France, the United Kingdom, Germany, Italy, and other major arms exporters, but also China, Brazil, and India, and other new arms exporters, to work out new systems of control? Did he have any notion of how difficult it would be for the rich to give up this profitable trade? Did he understand how reluctant the poor might be to do so? Indeed, did he understand how infinitely more complex such multilateral negotiations would be than any undertaken on a bilateral basis with the Soviet Union since the early 1960s, when the first negotiations on a test ban treaty suggested that other arms control measures might eventually be taken?

The President alluded to no such plans. Indeed, both he and his Secretary of State were incapable of comprehending the enormous efforts that would have to be made to regulate the sale of arms, to distinguish between offensive and defensive systems, to institute surveillance systems to guarantee that defensive systems were not technologically transformed so as to give the purchaser offensive capabilities. Such matters greatly exceeded the intellectual interests and political energies of the President. More importantly, they transcended his understanding of what the putative end of the Cold War portended. In his mind, its significance seemed to lie only in the fact that the Soviet Union, in its diminished power, would no longer be a major military rival of the United States, seeking clients in the world and supplying them with the commodity they most coveted, arms. That all this was wishful thinking, that the Soviet Union, desperate for hard currency, might continue to be interested in the arms trade, and might indeed be a competitor of the United States in that trade, and not only in the sale of second-hand weapons, seems never to have occurred to him. That new instabilities would be created by arms, and not only in the Middle East, was so remote from his thinking as not to be mentioned.

Failing to imagine what the new post-Cold War world would be, he could do no more than continue with the policies of his Republican predecessors. His Secretary of State would make the peace that had eluded Shultz. His policies vis-à-vis the Soviet Union would be those of Ronald Reagan. The President never asked whether such policies in 1991 or 1992 would have the relevance they were thought to have in 1987 or 1988. It was not so much his not being able to predict what was likely to happen in Moscow—a President served by intelligence services unable to warn him of a coming Iraqi invasion of Kuwait was not likely to be well advised on changes impending in the Kremlin—but his being unable to comprehend the significance of what had already happened in the Soviet Union and in the larger Communist world outside. In his repetition of slogans, he missed the opportunity to make distinctions, to understand what had in fact died in the Soviet Union, and what was still alive, though not necessarily vital or resilient.

On one level, the end of the Cold War meant the disintegration of the Warsaw Pact, which gave new freedom not only to the former Communist regimes of Central and Eastern Europe but also to all NATO members. The President was as lacking in ideas about what to do with NATO—other than to keep it going—as the Soviet President was in thinking about the future of the Soviet Union. In the American failure to understand how much the whole Middle Eastern situation had been altered by the Soviet "collapse"—if so dramatic a term could be used—the President appreciated only what the display of American military power in the area probably meant to the Soviets, and not only to their military leaders. He did not grasp how it had altered the political and military equation in the area, and indeed in the world.

If Arab states had been genuinely fearful of Soviet incursions—if Sadat's notion of a Communist pincers movement had not been sheer fantasy, if indeed it guided him in his move toward better understanding with both the United States and Israel  that specific hazard had evaporated. What, then, was the threat in the Gulf, if it no longer came from the Soviet Union or Soviet-spawned and Soviet-supported governments? Would the planned joint exercises with Saudi Arabia be calculated to thwart potential Iranian invasion, with Iran becoming the enemy again, in the manner of Iraq? Did the President believe that Iran was still determined to export fundamentalist Islamic revolution in the Middle East and that naval power could impede that export? Or did he expect his naval power to protect Kuwait should the opposition forces in that country become a serious threat to the emir?

Or did he really believe, as he implied, that the conditions were now propitious for peace in Lebanon, and that his talented Secretary of State would in fact be able to do a great deal to restore that shattered society? Was it the American victory in the Gulf that created this situation? Was it the reduced power of the Soviets in the region that would make Syria more accommodating? Had the humbling of the PLO, the serious blows to Arafat personally, created new opportunities in Lebanon, and if so, what precisely did he hope to do there? When he spoke so blithely of that country, of finding "solutions to the problem in Lebanon," never defining the problem, but proposing to take up the agenda that his predecessor had so totally fumbled with, did he have any notion of what that problem was? Did he consult prominent Lebanese-Americans, in his entourage or in the Senate, to find out what more than a decade of civil war and foreign intervention had done to reduce that society to penury, in comparison to what it had once been?

Could President Bush, who had attended the National Security Council meetings that made the Reagan administration's major decisions about American policy in Lebanon, ever understand why foreign policy on the cheap, which would never involve sacrifice or loss of American lives, could never succeed in the Middle East?

In the millions of words uttered in the American media on the disgrace of Iran-Contra, all attention was focused on what the deception said about the White House. President Reagan's own presidential fortunes—his ability to surmount the inquest into the affair—had preoccupied the media to the neglect of another issue, perhaps less vital, but still important. How did the whole miserable incident play in the Middle East, and particularly in Iran, not to speak of Iraq? What did all this secret American toadying to the Iranians, the shameless bargaining of arms for hostages, and the pretense of not doing it at all reveal about the United States? What did Arabs learn about American honor, American truthfulness, but most importantly, about American resolve? President Reagan, preoccupied with the hostages, had imagined that any covert policies calculated to achieve their release were justified. The Vice President, in his own accommodating way, had agreed. Neither understood why the hostage issue could never be allowed to determine Middle East policy, that while it was a sensitive issue at home, with great political implications, there were other, far more pressing matters in the Middle East.

That the President had stopped the war when he did, that he silenced General Schwarzkopf when the desert hero suggested that the cease-fire may have been premature, that he ought to have been allowed to go into Baghdad and take Saddam prisoner, was part and parcel of a larger strategic error that no Republican dared acknowledge and that no Democrat knew how to exploit. The President had imagined that to enter Baghdad was to make the mistake the Israelis had made in entering West Beirut: it would lead to loss of American lives, perhaps to wholly unacceptable numbers of American casualties. Given that prospect, and the understandable concern to give no further offense to the Soviet Union—to keep to the strict letter of the United Nations Security Council resolutions—it made sense for the American President to declare the cease-fire when he did. What it would mean for the people of Iraq, for the Shiite minority, what it might mean for the Kurds, the most threatened ethnic group in that unhappy land, scarcely concerned him.

When the President came in triumph to address the American Congress, the Kurd flight had not yet become a human disaster, attracting world attention. No mention was made of any such dire prospect, since it was not taken in by those who inhabited a White House still wreathed in its yellow colors. Later, when it did happen, unnamed administration sources would blame the United Nations for its slowness in sending help. The United States, however unwittingly, had contributed to the disaster, but wished only to leave it. Others were expected to clean it up, as others would clean up the oil slick in the Gulf, long forgotten, and douse the fires burning in the oil wells of Kuwait. The United States, always prepared to offer its expert guidance in all such technologically complex operations, could not imagine a larger (or more hazardous) role for itself. With the desire to avoid responsibility came the most egregious new self-praise; only the American Army was able rapidly to provide the tent shelter the nearly one million Kurds in their misery required; in no time at all, purified water and the dispatch of food and medicines would diminish their death toll. In any case, there was no American responsibility for what had happened to them. It was all Saddam's wicked doing.

This was the whole story of the Gulf War. The President could never acknowledge that in choosing war he had inflicted death, not so much on Americans, whom he confidently expected not to die in great number, as on thousands of others, trapped in the area. He could never understand what the presiding bishop of his own Episcopal Church had tried to tell him the day before he sent his airplanes and missiles into Iraq and Kuwait. The Most Reverend Edmond Browning, phoning the President, pleaded with him to desist; "I do not think war is the answer to this situation," the bishop said. There was no reason for the President to heed that call any more than there was reason for earlier Presidents to listen to the bishops of the Catholic Church or of any of the Protestant sects who at one time or other urged caution. Yet, in his failure, in his moral obtuseness, in his total preoccupation with political success, in his failure to understand how the world had changed since

Richard Nixon inhabited the White House, the President showed himself, for all his privileged background, the political heir of Ronald Reagan. The Gulf War would be Grenada, Libya, and Panama, though on a vastly larger scale, and with much greater consequences. Those who huddled around the President and helped plan the Gulf operations knew that the Soviet Union was weak, that it was not in a position to thwart him.

The President's initial failure to perceive the demise of *perestroika*, already evident to those who knew the Soviet Union in 1989, allowed him to take advantage of Gorbachev a year later when everyone recognized the Soviet President's weakness. While those who remembered 1939 grieved for Lithuania, Latvia, and Estonia, and raised their voices against Kremlin policies that appeared dangerously repressive, the President remained silent. His ambition told him that there was no profit in standing for Baltic independence, let alone Ukrainian autonomy. His habit was always to take the easy course, the one calculated to help him electorally. His was not a geopolitical intelligence, which sought to imagine the world of 2020; like most American politicians, he calculated only in four-year units. Because Saddam was an aggressor and a murderer, though neither a Hitler nor a Stalin, if only because he lacked their more ample human and material resources, he was the ideal enemy for the American President, particularly so when the Soviet President was otherwise engaged, seeking to maintain law and order in the republics. Having no real opposition abroad, and none in Congress, which scarcely divined his plans, he moved majestically ahead to do precisely what he wanted; he had his war.

The President had no idea of how the world regarded the United States. Who would tell him the truth? Who would tell him that his Secretary of State's capacity to fashion a coalition and keep it together for more than a few months was something less than a very remarkable diplomatic achievement, that it added nothing to the repute of democracy in the world, that it gave the United States no permanent new resource that it could avail itself of in the future? It could not even be translated into a plea for more generous aid to the Kurds. Who would tell him that Communism, once thought to be a threat in Africa, had virtually disappeared from that ravaged continent, but that the authoritarian regimes, under new colors, and under their old flags, continued? Who would instruct him about India and Indonesia, vast societies that he knew nothing about, that had not gained new respect for the United States because it had humbled a rogue named Saddam Hussein?

Yet what difference did it make? The Bush administration was prepared to do nothing even in Eastern Europe—to preach the benefits of a free market economy, of course, always mentioning the blessings of democracy—but showing itself incapable of fashioning a policy suited to the 1990s. To try to work in harness with the European Community—largely lost in its own agenda, seeking to resolve its monetary union questions before 1992—the President would have had to take initiatives comparable to those once taken by Truman and Eisenhower. It would have required him to become familiar with a world he knew nothing about, whose experience with "free markets" in the 1920s, Fascism in the 1930s, Nazism and Communism in the 1940s—to give only the most superficial rendering of its more recent past—would have demanded empathy and imagination, qualities in short supply.

The President's conservatism lay not in his theories and even less in his policies; he had none worthy of so honorable a name. His habit was to wait, hoping for something to turn up. He scarcely knew what to do in 1989, the year of revolutions; he was no more fleet of foot in 1990, the year of Gorbachev's repressions. When, in 1991, Yeltsin achieved his remarkable electoral success in Russia, he received the ex-Communist in the White House more cordially than he had some years previously, still not knowing what to do or say. His failure to conceive of a generous policy for nations making their exit from Communism as earlier administrations had done with those making their exit from Fascism and military rule—Spain, Portugal, and Greece, for example—reflected more than a disdain for what he so casually dismissed as that "vision thing."

Yet he believed that his Gulf victory had transformed the world. The idea that the political problems of Nicaragua, Peru, the Philippines, Egypt, Algeria, Pakistan, and Kenya, the plight of billions of poor in Asia, Africa, Latin America, and the Middle East were in some way affected by what he had done seemed implicit in his rhetoric. His currency was cheap, pro-testations of goodwill, words and promises, unlikely in them-selves to reduce world disorder. No one suggested that the President's task was to draw up a blueprint for the 1990s, or to deputize others to do this for him. If his obligation was to provide leadership, giving heed to the traditional Christian injunction that "the truth will make you free," there was an even more compelling constitutional injunction that required him to share power, to expect and respect opposition. Was it possible for him even to entertain the possibility that the world had become more precarious, not less so, that it was a more dangerous place in the 1990s than it had been in the 1950s, that the end of the Cold War made it so?

His political script was much too sanguine. If the disappear-ance of the Soviet Union as a prime mover in international affairs reduced one threat, others had taken root. Economic discontent, both at home and abroad, fueled by new expecta-tions and amplified by systems of communication which mocked all pretense of social harmony and progress, created a poten-tially explosive political mixture, and not only in the few places that had figured in the television commentary of 1991. For those who were themselves comfortable, who esteemed a na-tion's strength simply by its capacity to raise and maintain a military force, the reasons for the "decline and fall" of the Soviet empire had never been understood. The moral issues

raised by popular dissent meant little to men who judged all
things in economic terms—who had no sense of the nature of
either religious or nationalist passion. The concern with halting
an aggressor, replaying the script of the 1930s, diverted attention from the corrosive effects of a new social virus—rampant
nationalism—relatively dormant for decades, contained by
Cold War rivalry and rhetoric.

The Gulf adventure harmed the country, not least by diverting it from its real economic and political problems, not
only domestically but also in the foreign field. It allowed for
new playacting. When President Bush visited Greece in July—
the first President to do so since Eisenhower in 1959—he
proclaimed his intention to act, to show what the New World
Order meant, and to do so at once. In announcing that he
would seek to alter the status of Cyprus, resolving a problem
that had plagued relations between NATO allies for decades,
he assumed the role he loved, the honest broker, the peacemaker. As his Secretary of State dashed off to Syria, intent on
convening the peace conference that would settle disputes that
had generated such tragic war and violence, it seemed that the
Gulf success was indeed creating a new role for the United
States. The President, in responding to the entreaties of the
Greek Prime Minister "to get involved in the Cyprus problem,"
was simply doing what America did best, what it had done so
frequently in the past. It was a challenging opportunity, but
*The New York Times* reported also, almost parenthetically, that
"the Greek armed forces have a long shopping list to buy jet
fighters, warships, tanks and other equipment," and that the
President had said that it is "our intention to do what we can
to strengthen the Greek armed forces." To accomplish what?
To fight whom? No one asked.

The way to the hearts of Greeks, it would appear, was the
way to the hearts of Arabs, Israelis, and all manner of others
who recognized, more than ever, perhaps because of the Gulf
War, the superiority of American arms. What, then, had

become of the need to "control the proliferation of weapons
of mass destruction and the missiles used to deliver them"?
Had the President in the heat of an Athens July forgotten his
words of March before the United States Congress? There had
been no forgetting. The President, even without the benefit of
a Cold War, lived by principles he had first learned in the
service of Richard Nixon, which had served him so well in all
the intervening years. He found it as difficult to make a
fundamental U-turn in foreign policy as any number of those
who continued to have offices in the Kremlin, at least before
the attempted August coup. Better relations with the Soviet
Union did not translate into developing an industrial policy
that might make the United States less economically dependent
on the sale of arms. It did not require him to fashion policies
that would dramatically improve the American work force,
which he declared incomparable, having proved itself with its
Patriot missiles.

　Defined by his World War II experience, and even more by
all that the Cold War had taught him, the President lived by
myth, greatly exaggerating his own accomplishments, imagining that a White House tenancy, particularly if it was renewed,
gave evidence of his remarkable talents as a diplomat. The
reality was otherwise; he knew the game of American politics,
as Ronald Reagan played it; his understanding of international
relations was minimal. He pretended that the decline of the
Soviet Union simply reinvigorated and made even more intimate his relations with all his NATO allies. No one had ever
told him that there were no permanent alliances. He imagined
that Germany would for all time thank him for what he had
done to restore unity, as it would remain forever grateful for
what the United States had done to defeat Nazism and contain
Communism. He saw foreign states as static entities, when all
the evidences of his lifetime suggested the opposite. Not
everyone in Eastern and Central Europe waited to be "developed" by the new united Germany, not everyone in the Soviet

Union had forgiven or forgotten World War II or imagined that only their Communist rulers had oppressed them. Historical memories were long—Arabs still spoke of the Sykes-Picot pact—and the Japanese thought of Hiroshima in a way that American psychologists never could. The whole history of the twentieth century suggested that the most stable and seemingly permanent features of life were in fact transitory. The President, having little historical perspective, scarcely understood this, failing to see the opportunities created by a whole set of events that gave the United States a much enlarged scope for global action, of a kind it had never previously contemplated.

The principal challenge for the United States was not to become the world's policeman, organizing friendly (and not so friendly) nations to fight territorial aggression, or even instructing them in how to make peace—to do in the 1990s what it sometimes immodestly pretended to have done persistently in the past—but to assume a new role, to see itself as the quintessential "modern society," divided and fractious, a microcosm of global society, with all its racial and cultural conflicts and divisions. The old sort of Cold War Manichaeanism, with its simple good guy/bad guy divisions, had reduced all political debate to television drivel; it had coarsened social sensibility and made American society vulgar. More seriously, it had forced the United States to repudiate its long-standing utopian ambition—to be democratic and open.

If the United States today includes tens of thousands of homeless, millions who are impoverished, and tens of millions denied the health and family care that any civilized European Community member believes to be a democratic citizen's due, it is not because the facts are unknown, or because the society is cursed with a population indolent and uninspired, unwilling to make the effort that would create the universal prosperity and good feeling that are said to exist in those places spared such social calamities. Nor can it be seriously argued that the fault is with the electorate, with a Republican Party that has managed to impose itself on the nation, appealing particularly to white males of every social class, speaking in a racist code that is sanitized, only faintly resembling the one the Democratic Party used to retain its power in the South after the Civil War. The flaws are much deeper; they reflect an unwillingness to confront certain realities which touch at the very heart of the American dilemma—how to acknowledge that decades of Cold War transformed the nation, making it less moral, less innovative, and only superficially more motivated to address its fundamental social problems.

Whether or not Gorbachev survives as the President of a viable Soviet Union, whether or not Baker succeeds in pressuring Israel "to give peace a chance," the new world, a disordered world, will be one of nationalist resurgence and religious intolerance, of economic and social inequities that produce violent explosions, made all the more incendiary when restrictive immigration policies are introduced in many places in Europe and elsewhere to remove a safety valve provided by the more prosperous to those they wish to employ in menial pursuits. The world is more dangerous not because Communism has failed but because decades of Cold War have raised ambitions, and not only in Europe.

Beyond all these hazards, however, and they can be easily multiplied, lurks an even greater danger: that the United States will itself not be able to put its own house in order, that the disruptions following from this failure will affect the world more fundamentally and more permanently than anything produced by the collapse of the Communist utopia. The United States refuses to take in what a Soviet friend, Sergei Kapitsa, out of courtesy to his American hosts, chooses not to say too openly: if the Cold War is indeed over, as "highest authority" insists it is, and if the Soviet Union is the "main loser," with Japan and Germany the principal winners, where is the United States? The possibility that it, too, has lost, though in a very different way, is what the Soviet scientist refuses to say. His meaning, however, is clear.

An American, reflecting on this, may wish to draw different

conclusions from four decades of the Cold War. Is it at all possible that there have been no victors, that Germany and Japan, despite their very real economic prosperity, represent nothing that has ultimate meaning for the world? Might the dilemma of the late twentieth century be that the American utopia has lost its authority at precisely the same time that the Soviet myth has been smashed and that their simultaneous collapse creates a grave intellectual and ethical vacuum in the world? If so, what can that mean to those concerned with the United States, with its future political and moral role in the world? Will they acknowledge that the Cold War, perhaps necessary, contributed to the defeat of Soviet Communism, but also served to create many of the least attractive features of late-twentieth-century American (and world) society? More importantly, is it possible that five decades of war, beginning in 1941, have instructed the American people in a flawed text, that they imagine foreign policy and domestic policy to be separable, that one may be successful in one and fail in the other? In truth, they are related, in ways that neither Bush nor Reagan could ever understand. Unless President Bush's foreign policy is placed in a context that includes his failure to address the serious domestic problems of the United States, and not only of the American economy, there is no possibility of the country emerging from the current era of fable and myth.

While the President's failure to enunciate new foreign policies adequate to the twenty-first century reflects his own personal limitations, the failure of the society to generate such discussion reflects a more serious fault: if the Republican Party made the White House a myth factory, the Democratic Party has been no more successful in keeping alive certain traditions in the Congress, where Senators and Representatives, with their much expanded staffs, were unable to bridle presidential pride and pretension. There is no need to suggest that all was better in the first or the middle decades of the century. What has to be acknowledged is that the President's performance before, during, and after the Gulf War—and the nation's blithe acceptance of that performance—suggests a serious national disorder which will not be remedied simply by the arrival of a more able man (or woman) in the White House. Something has happened to the republic, and there is no way to ignore the danger it poses to the future peace and well-being of the country and also of the world. The greatest of the world's democracies has lost its way, in foreign policy and in domestic policy. It no longer knows what is important, no longer exercises judgment, no longer mocks pretense. Worse, it no longer recognizes tragedy, having cheapened even that resource.

In his celebratory New World Order speech, the President urged Congress to "move forward aggressively on our domestic front." Using the hundred-day legislative deadline made famous by an earlier President in 1933, whose name went unmentioned, the President asked for the Congress to agree quickly on a transportation and crime bill. If "our forces," he said, "could win the ground war in a hundred hours, then surely the Congress can pass this legislation in a hundred days." The President spoke of honoring all Americans, of whatever race, creed, or color, who had served so ably in the Gulf War; he asked the nation to do this by "setting its face against discrimination, bigotry and hate." This was the message about race relations from the man who made Willie Horton famous, who resisted all efforts to enact new civil rights legislation.

There were only two other substantive comments. The President, seeing the Americans as a "caring people," went on to say: "We are a good people, a generous people. Let us always be caring and good and generous in all we do."

After the great victory in the Gulf War, the President had his first chance to unveil his proposed educational reforms. With an able new Secretary of Education at his side, Lamar Alexander, a replacement for the less gifted secretary whom the President had inherited and somewhat unceremoniously discarded, he spoke of the days of the status quo as being over. Again, the "points of light"—so vivid a metaphor—appeared in his prepared remarks, but in the new secretary's words, this was not just a program, but a "crusade." To show his own command of history, the President added: "There will be no renaissance without revolution," and nothing less than both was promised. The nation would wish to know that the President intended to participate personally in the "educational renaissance" by himself learning to operate a computer!

The administration promised to establish at least 535 experimental schools—one for each House district and two for each state—and to have these operating by 1996. They were to provide incentives for educational experiment. Each "New American School" would be given $1 million in seed money; after that, they would have to become self-supporting, with public or private money. But this was not all. The President's plan included provisions for more traditional schools where parents, teachers, schools, and communities would be encouraged to evaluate the results of a battery of new tests, to determine how individual students and schools were doing. If they were not measuring up, pressure could be exerted by one or other of these constituencies to force change. There would be new nationwide (though voluntary) tests in five core subjects—English, mathematics, science, geography, and history—and colleges would be encouraged to consult these test scores, as would all prospective employers. Those students who did exceptionally well in these tests would be awarded Presidential Citations for Educational Excellence.

For those who did well but required financial assistance, there would be Presidential Achievement Scholarships to colleges and universities. Not only would report cards go to parents to tell them how their children were doing, but information on the academic achievements of individual schools, school districts, and all states would be made public. Indeed, there would be a national report card, periodically issued, to show how the country as a whole was doing. Beginning in 1994, data would be collected and published on student performance in grades four, eight, and twelve in all five core subjects. For a parent who saw that his or her child was being educationally shortchanged, the right, indeed the incentive, to transfer to another school would exist. In his "populist crusade" to reform education, the President was invoking the great need for parent power. Individual schools would be rewarded if they improved markedly; they would be given what amounted to federal bounties.

Nothing less than a "New Generation of American Schools" was promised. Without drawing historical parallels, the federal government at the end of the twentieth century pretended to be doing for schools what had been done for higher education in 1862 with the Morrill Act. New kinds of institutions were going to be created, with federal support. The only difference was that the land-grant colleges created in the middle of the Civil War were supported with real resources, land owned by the federal government. There were no comparable appropriations in the Bush plan. The country was expected to know that the federal government had neither monetary nor other resources to distribute. Still, as a token of goodwill and good intention, there was the promise of $1 million to each new school.

Secretary Alexander asked that there be no hasty judgments on the President's plan. His words were significant: "There will be no silver bullets, there will be no miracles, there will be no great transformation by the next presidential election." Who had ever suggested that there might be? What educational reformer had ever imagined that America's schools could be remade in cighteen months? Yet the secretary's words revealed a mind-set in the Bush administration more significant than almost anything the President himself said.

For those who recognized in the emptiness of the prose more than just a failure to commit real resources—billions of federal dollars—the whole scheme could be dismissed as another obeisance to testing, to what a concern with "skills and drills" was expected to achieve, and never would. But the initial response was fairly muted, both from those who emerged as the President's supporters and from those who dismissed the efforts as much ado about nothing, failing to show any proper concern for the millions of children who would never be affected by it. Much of the response, in reflecting either the hope that at last the President was committing himself to education or the fear that the plan addressed all the wrong issues, failed to see the larger significance of what the President had done.

He was preparing himself for 1992. The man who had come into the White House saying he intended to be the nation's "Education President" was fulfilling his pledge. The effort was a fraud, from beginning to end, but no one discovered political or educational advantages in saying so. The failure of the President's program derived neither from its fiscal federal stinginess—all would depend ultimately on the states; the federal government, as Americans knew, was "bankrupt"—nor from its obviously narrow definition of schooling and learning. The failure lay deeper, in its intellectual and pedagogical aridity, in its failure to understand the dimensions of the social and economic crises that had transformed the country, in its unwillingness to acknowledge that the youth of America in the last decade of the century scarcely resembled those who lived in pre-World War II America.

The President himself lived in a mythical world, or at least pretended to. Had he sent a trusted deputy to visit his old school for just a few hours, he would have learned much that would have dismayed him, a great deal that might have instructed him. It was not the Phillips Andover of 1942, and not only or principally because of co-education. The famed Phillips spirit, in its 1940s form, was gone; so, also, was the old-style faculty. Turnover was constant, and morale was said to be low, but not because students avoided brute fact, thinking it unnecessary. The school infirmary, in providing information about sex, did not advertise its policies on condom distribution nor did it wish to discuss the advice it offered to those seeking an abortion. If the President could neither understand nor tolerate new mores and habits in a privileged enclave like that of Phillips Andover, how could he even begin to imagine the situation in the public schools of Hartford and Houston, not to speak of those in New York and Washington? Still, he and those who advised him on school reform imagined that some version of 1942 education was recoverable, mostly through exhortation and testing.

The President, unable to utter the word "blacks" in speaking about the country's educational dilemmas any more than he had been able to speak of Israel or Iran as he went about preparing for his Gulf War, wished to live in the comfortable and beguiling 1940s Hollywood version of America, with its God-fearing and God-loving peoples pursuing innocent pleasures. While certain prominent educators and politicians hailed the President's educational strategy as a "bold departure," claiming that it might in time rival the great educational initiatives of Lyndon Johnson, their words reflected nothing so much as an unwillingness to see the President for what he was. President Bush understood neither reform nor revolution; he had no idea of what a renaissance in education would be. Responding to a real crisis—perhaps the most urgent in the society—he came forward with phrases and bureaucratic gimmicks, all cost-free.

The United States had become a victim of years of self-neglect, self-delusion, and self-praise. Once a quintessential model of a progressive society, it had become dowdy and old-fashioned, losing appreciation of its one remaining substantial resource—the heterogeneity of its people. The New World Order, much touted during and after the Gulf War, particularly by triumphalists who scarcely understood what more than four decades of Cold War had done to change American society, lacked specific content precisely because those who were its ardent advocates refused to gaze on conditions as they were, and could not begin to imagine conditions as they might be. The United States fell into a trough where code words drove out criticism, and nostalgia substituted for civic virtue.

This was apparent during the months leading up to the Gulf War, became even more obvious during the weeks of the war, and took on yet new dimensions in the months that followed. If no one called this a "postwar," perhaps out of a sense of the ludicrousness of attaching such a grandiose name to so modest an undertaking, it did not prevent the society from continuing to celebrate. The original celebrations, scheduled for July 4, were advanced, perhaps out of a fear that the nostalgia would not survive. New York, impoverished, drug-ridden, and phys-ically decaying, pretended again to be the center of a nation that recalled, however vaguely, what ticker tape showered on conquering heroes had once meant in pictorial display, even in a pre-television age. While the ticker tape no longer existed, and much else had changed since the time of Lindbergh, the city put on its extravagant show, and the suburban office workers crowded in. Like so much else in the new age, the event cost the city nothing; wealthy businessmen, chief execu-tive officers, distinguished lawyers, passed the hat around in their corporate boardrooms to give the crowds their "circuses," providing the conquering heroes the welcome they deserved.

One other incident—less happy—marred this period. The hospitalization of the President for a rapid heartbeat, soon diagnosed as Graves' disease, and accompanied with a loss of weight, obvious fatigue, slurred speech and occasional memory lapses, created limited panic but directed attention to the Vice President, Dan Quayle, who sat only a heartbeat away from becoming head of state. Questions were raised about how this middle-aged boy had come to be chosen by the President in the first instance, but no one said the obvious. There was something seriously amiss in a political system that allowed a presidential nominee such latitude in choosing the individual who, at least in the twentieth century, had such an excellent chance of becoming President of the United States. Some suggested that the President might wish to reconsider his vice-presidential choice in 1992, as Dwight Eisenhower had reconsidered his in 1956, but there was no obvious replacement. James Baker was ineligible; his Texas residence precluded his being taken on in 1992. In any case, his own political game plan required him to continue till 1996, when active service as Secretary of State would make him the obvious choice against a figurehead Vice President who had done little. If fate intervened to make Quayle president before that, Baker might wish to challenge him as Robert Kennedy had once thought to challenge Lyndon Johnson, his candidate's choice as Vice President, who had then succeeded to the presidency. The Reagan-Bush era would be perpetuated, for those who believed in it, into the twenty-first century.

No one argued in these terms in the spring of 1991 when the "dog days" of summer came early, and the mass media amused themselves in recounting the tale of the ways in which another heavy, the former Governor of New Hampshire, used White House transport for private travel, emphasizing his need as Chief of Staff to remain in constant and secure communication with the White House. These capers vied with more serious matters, the sad plight of the Kurds and the Shiites in Iraq, the discovery that Saddam retained some sort of nuclear capability, or at least was thought to have such, and the growing realization that a territorial objective—to free Kuwait from Iraq's dictator—had not sufficed to make Iraq submissive, the area secure.

However newsworthy such events proved to be—for a week, a fortnight, or longer—they could not possibly vie with a more consequential happening which gradually came to hold center stage. As Gorbachev moved away from his harder line, as

Yeltsin achieved his impressive electoral victory, there were demands, both in the United States and abroad, that the world's industrial democracies do more to help the Soviet Union, specifically to assist its beleaguered, reform-minded President, who had done so much to liberate East Europe. In the European Community, Germany took the lead among those who feared the consequences of an economic and political explosion in the Soviet Union that might lead millions to seek refuge abroad, creating insuperable problems for all Europe, particularly Germany, the richest neighbor. Fear created the imperative for action; hope, however, fueled it. Germany, recalling the influence it had enjoyed for centuries in the Russia of the tsars, saw vast economic and political opportunities for itself in reasserting a traditional friendship with a less developed state, European and Asian. While the rehabilitation of East Germany was expected to consume substantial German capital for a very long time, a decade or more, Germany was considering also the world of the twenty-first century. It did so not by thinking in the romantic late-nineteenth- and early-twentieth-century terms of a Berlin-Baghdad connection, or of greater efforts in underdeveloped Africa, but in the more beguiling idiom of the days of Peter the Great and a number of his successors, of Berlin-Moscow ties.

Meanwhile, in the United States, those who still carried great expectations of what the Soviet President might one day be able to do as head of state worried principally about the stability of his regime. Their fear was less of economic and political disorder that might send millions teeming into Central and Western Europe, and more of what would happen to its vast stock of thermonuclear weapons should disorder and chaos ensue. The problem of "command and control," so critical for so large a stockpile of lethal arms, quite apart from any sympathy for Gorbachev himself, suggested that the United States should do more to help him. When a group of Harvard academics sought to do so, concocting an ambitious program of aid, doing so in collaboration with a small group of Soviet reform-minded economists, the Bush administration, through Lawrence Eagleburger, disparaged the effort and disdained the academic meddling. It was one thing for the government to recruit Harvard academics to seek to make peace in Vietnam, as President Johnson did with another Harvard academic, Henry Kissinger, to whom Deputy Secretary Eagleburger was much beholden, but it was quite another thing for a group of Harvard academics, entrepreneurs, to go off on their own, having no understanding of either the politics or the geopolitics of the region.

The Bush administration did not welcome interference from outsiders, neither from politicians like Mitterrand who sought vainly to involve France and the European Community in persuading Saddam to negotiate in the early months after the invasion, nor from European and American academic experts who knew Iraq intimately but were never seriously consulted while the war was proceeding, and least of all from those who imagined that their kind of knowledge substituted for what the administration knew from speaking face-to-face with Gorbachev and two Soviet Foreign Ministers for more than half a decade. Behind the dismissal of academic meddling—of no great consequence in itself—lay a White House political strategy that almost no one commented on. The Bush administration lacked a policy for dealing with the Soviet Union in 1989; it had none worthy of the name in 1990, though it recognized how Soviet weakness could translate into a political advantage in the Gulf War; it still lacked such a policy in 1991. Politics required, however, that this fact be hidden. In the New World Order that was being heralded, the Soviet Union would have its place, as co-convener of a Middle East peace conference.

As for extending greater aid, with resources that did not exist, the President could do nothing to keep Gorbachev from coming to London, from pushing his way into the meeting of the Group of Seven, from stealing the media show, but he could do a great deal to guarantee that he went away empty-handed, for all the promises made, and that the occasion would be the stage for the announcement of a new Soviet-American summit, later in the month, in Moscow, to seal the strategic arms treaty that had been consummated after nine years of unremitting toil. Again, photo opportunities would be provided, not with a cast of ten, as in London, but with only two, the greats, Bush and Gorbachev. The President knew how to manage his affairs; the greater question was whether he knew how to manage those of the country he presided over.

In fact, this was an open question, but few raised it in the aftermath of his success in the Gulf, in London and Moscow, in Athens and Istanbul, made even more impressive by the Secretary of State's almost equally dazzling accomplishments in Damascus and Amman. The President rode high, and few asked embarrassing questions, none calculated to puncture the fable he was creating. The world had passed out of a more than four-decades-long Cold War, as destructive in its own way, though not in human casualties, as Armageddon had been, the war that had ravaged Europe between 1914 and 1918. Men acted as if the damage done the Soviet Union and its satellite empire could be repaired, not immediately perhaps, but certainly, if only those making their exit from Communism recognized the necessity to convert quickly to a market economy. No one asked why the United States—one of the more ancient of the market economies, one that could almost claim a patent on the institution—continued to show signs of economic distress and social disorder. If the system worked so well, why did it not operate as effectively in the United States as it did in Germany and Japan, the new model industrial societies? No one thought it necessary to review the history of the nineteenth century, which would have explained how Socialism developed initially in response to certain inequities created by an unregulated free market economy, or how that economy had been superseded by state controls during the war, and how desperate had been the efforts to re-create it in 1919, to recapture a world that had been lost.

It was John Maynard Keynes, in *The Economic Consequences of the Peace*, written six months after the end of the war, who first announced that all such efforts were doomed to failure. The innocent pre-1914 capitalist world was not recoverable; too much had happened to create new appetites, not only for material goods but also for social protection, for men ever to accept again the discipline of self-denial they had tolerated in the nineteenth century when free market institutions allowed for unprecedented European (and American) industrial growth. In the last decade of the twentieth century, the European Community lived with the knowledge that it was economically prosperous and socially responsible, at least in providing for its own citizens. If the Soviet Union and others recently liberated from their Communist shackles encouraged foreign investment, liberated their markets, suppressed controls, they, too, could experience all the benefits of late-twentieth-century democracy. The European economic patent—that of Paris and Berlin, of Milan and Brussels—was offered the countries of Central and Eastern Europe with no one asking the question why the United States continued to be so backward, why it too did not see the wisdom of the West European way and adopt it.

The Bush administration never asked such questions, refusing to acknowledge the country's backwardness. Its own success depended on a single fable being believed by the electorate— that all went well in America, that it continued to be a teacher to the world, a moral example to others. The possibility that it had lost those distinctions, that its leadership was of a kind different from what it pretended, was never bruited about in or near the White House. To have acknowledged such failure would have required the construction of another political agenda very different from that of the New World Order. It would have asked, in all innocence, why social and economic conditions in the United States were so different from those across the border in Canada, so different from any in Germany and Japan. The United States lived with the "third world" within its borders; other nations, without such problems, aware of their good fortune, compensated by committing what they thought were substantial sums to the less privileged, who lived at a distance, abroad. It would have been churlish to tell the new rich nations that their "third world" investments were derisory, puny, that poverty and violence in Africa and Asia, in Latin America and elsewhere, while they derived not from centuries of imperialism, as some insisted, were not remediable by United Nations aid programs, or bilateral technical assistance schemes, conceived in the manner of the 1960s or 1970s. Nor would they be resolved by the simple introduction of free markets, the panacea offered the former Soviet empire, a nineteenth-century economic nostrum which claimed great potency.

But all such issues seemed strangely academic in the context of events in the Soviet Union in the week that began on Monday, August 19, that agitated the world for the next seventy-two hours. The coup against Mikhail Gorbachev, happily short-lived, produced results no one in the White House anticipated, the victory of Boris Yeltsin and the demise of Communism in the Soviet Union. These developments, prophesied years before at home and abroad by individuals not very partial to the Gorbachev enthusiasm common in Washington, required rethinking the Soviet scenario. In Bush–Baker circles, Yeltsin had been constantly underestimated; his arguments that *perestroika* was moribund, that Gorbachev was indecisive, that his commitment to democracy was limited, never sat well with those who imagined they knew the Soviet President intimately.

Yeltsin, who watched Gorbachev closely, was not overwhelmed by him. His appointments of Boris Pugo as Interior Minister and Valentin Pavlov as Prime Minister, both committed

Communists, together with Eduard Shevardnadze's resignation as Foreign Minister, and his very explicit warnings about an early return to Soviet totalitarianism, became the principal subjects of comment among all who styled themselves Russian democrats. In the White House, all such developments seemed inconsequential besides the infinitely more important ones occurring in the Gulf. Even the Soviet attacks on the Baltic republics raised only mild interest in a society transfixed by Iraq. Yeltsin understood that, between Gorbachev and himself, there could not be any contest, at least in the President's mind. Gorbachev was Bush's man, known, trusted, and prized. Yeltsin, an outsider, thought to be a demagogue or worse, led inchoate forces of small interest to American politicians, whose eyes were fixed on the Kremlin, not on the streets of Moscow.

In the circumstances, the American President showed a certain fleetness of foot in the August coup days. From one hour to the next, he forgot his earlier misgivings about the President of the Russian Republic, and saw him as a hero poised on a tank outside Moscow's White House. Again, he pretended to omniscience; all was going precisely as he always hoped it would. No reporter, on the golf links of Maine, asked the President whether his views on the Soviet Union had changed at all since his inaugural in January 1989. No one questioned him closely on whether he had not misperceived Gorbachev's ability to sustain the Soviet Union or to introduce democracy. The times were too grave for an American Boris Yeltsin to appear in either the Democratic or the Republican Party, mocking the pretensions of a man who preferred to follow events, rarely able to anticipate them, never causing them to happen. The President lacked a long-term foreign-affairs strategy; there was no one about prepared to say so, modestly or accurately.

Committed to pursuing a politics of illusion, the President pretended that his telephone conversation with Yeltsin mattered. The really consequential fact, that he lacked any notion of how more than four decades of Cold War had transformed the United States, that this prevented him from knowing what he might do in a totally novel situation that called for long-range planning, was scarcely acknowledged. The fact that the Cold War, for all its happy ending, had inflicted grave damage on many institutions, including the presidency itself, would have seemed bizarre to someone who imagined that the office had never enjoyed such universal prestige. The United States was the only surviving superpower—that, for the President, was the only fact of world significance.

Theory had never been the President's principal strength. No one had ever instructed him in the casualties sustained by victors, even in wars that were relatively bloodless. The idea that the American presidency itself was a principal casualty of the Cold War was not something bruited about in the corridors of the White House. It would have been thought a preposterous notion by men who had no sense of history, no intellectual grasp of the time when the office was constructed to be one of dignity and magistracy, incorporating virtues suited to a republic, so different from the monarchies of Europe. The destruction of the world of Washington, Jefferson, and Madison by what were thought to be the requirements of the Cold War—conflict with a ruthless adversary—led to perverse results. In the secrecy that the Cold War generated, in the "dirty tricks" it justified, in the illusions it propagated, not least that the President literally held the destiny of the world in his hands, violence was done to the truth. That his finger on the button gave him substantial power was of course accurate; that it made him something of an icon, fawned on by those who agreed to be his servants, had more important constitutional implications. The media, alternating between awe of his power and contempt for his occasional transgressions, sometimes too blatant to be ignored, helped create the new political order, centered in an all-powerful White House.

The nation was infantilized by its Cold War experience.

White House politicians and the media cooperated to produce myths, rarely recognized as such. Various forms of sycophancy, common to those admitted to the presence, enjoying access to "the King's closet"—a concept known in all powerful monarchies—demeaned the office while exaggerating its authority. A man with such awesome responsibilities would need help, indeed management. The vastly expanded post-World War II White House staffs, the changed nature of Cabinet offices, and the many new multi-tiered federal bureaucracies guaranteed that those who served the President would indulge him in his vanities and fantasies, packaging both as rational public policies.

Congress, inevitably, suffered a loss of prestige. With such a political system,what could so undisciplined and amorphous a body do? The politics of the Cold War required some consultation, but Congress was increasingly thought to be almost peripheral, a nuisance, at least from the informed perspective of 1600 Pennsylvania Avenue. Dismissed as "Yahoos on the Hill," though never called that in public, members of Congress were seen as men and women who sought only to impede a hardworking executive with their impertinent interventions and perennial investigations. On the surface, a minimal courtesy prevailed; below, there was only contempt, artfully concealed. To callow men, elevated to great public stations and conscious only of where power lay, Congress appeared to be a collection of prima donnas who could be relied on mostly to know the value of the one currency they accepted, public monies for favored local projects, guaranteed to win constituent support. Congressional debates counted for nothing; committee hearings were more important, but only if they figured on television news in three-minute sound bites. Nothing that happened out of the sight of television cameras was important, by definition.

In these circumstances, the White House became the only show in town, with a small city on the Potomac suddenly elevated to the center of the universe. The damage done the nation by the Cold War was visible in government, but also in every city of the country, and nowhere more conspicuously than in the festering black ghettos of a society that still wished to see them as invisible. So long as a fiendish foreign enemy existed—faithless Communism—it was impossible for the White House to misconstrue the nation's first priority. The appointment of a black man or woman to a high post was thought significant, but in fact changed very little as the incidence of crime grew and evidences of drug abuse both among children and among adults became a national disgrace. The criminal justice system was said to be on the verge of collapse; a greatly expanded prison system seemed scarcely sufficient to accommodate unprecedented numbers of men, mostly black and young. The nation's public transport and health services were recognized to be in jeopardy, but these were small matters when compared with the decay of the nation's schools, all too often violent and unsafe, where many hundreds of thousands of children were warehoused, to keep them away for at least a few hours from the dangers of inner-city streets.

The same Manichaean idiom, to distinguish between the "evil empire" of the Soviet Union and the democratic republic across the Atlantic, was increasingly used to describe the population at home, divided between an industrious and virtuous majority and a reckless, indolent, and vice-ridden minority, who caused all the trouble. An older American style of political debate went out of fashion; the new style, created for use on television, depended on code words, especially significant at those crucial four-year intervals when the future of the nation was being decided. Melodrama became the staple of politics; humor was banished. To suggest that the White House had been recently used as a retirement home, that a minor tyrant was elevated to appear as a new Hitler, that a make-believe war, which could have had only one result militarily, was given more cosmic importance—and that these were the characteristic features of the new American politics—these were fairly serious charges, legitimated only by the fact that they were true, that they described a country governed by an executive increasingly given to staging media events, incapable of coping with serious revolutionary issues.

Roosevelt was courted by Churchill and Stalin because he was prepared to mobilize and share the produce of a self-confident society, recently emerged from a traumatic depression, but still unscathed by war. In his willingness to conscript, deploy, and risk armies and navies—asking for sacrifice from millions—Roosevelt recognized the importance of engaging the public. He had no interest in their mouthing popular patriotic sentiments, though he had no objection to them. Neither he nor his allies ever doubted that the margin between victory and defeat lay substantially in what the United States agreed to do, what the Congress and the people were to accept. The Second World War was dangerous for all who fought it, and not simply because Allied leaders announced that fact publicly.

During the early years of the Cold War, Truman and Eisenhower took other risks, no less fraught with consequences for the world, which saw the United States pitted against a power known to have atomic arms and thought to be militarily superior on the ground in its conventional weapons capability. Again, those who stood with the United States understood the gamble; they recognized that the stakes were high. The possibility of a tragic miscalculation on either side was known to exist. Real drama characterized these events, never staged for television viewing. Both Reagan and Bush, compelled to act on smaller stages, confronting insubstantial military foes never in a position to challenge them decisively, scarcely understood the real challenges of their day, at home or abroad. The Soviet Union's economic difficulties, already apparent in the first years of Reagan's administration, grew perceptibly. As the evidences of Soviet weakness multiplied, both Reagan and Bush were of course delighted; neither knew how to use these unprecedented and unexpected bonuses to the advantage of the American people, to provide an anchor for a new international system less committed to the use of arms, more sensitive to issues of equality.

Reagan and Bush lacked the experience, the intelligence, and the morality of the last great Republican Party president, Dwight Eisenhower. Neither had the capacity to plan, to anticipate problems; neither knew the importance of mobilizing the nation for major foreign policy innovations. Neither was a strategist; both were tacticians, preoccupied with themselves. When Eisenhower, in his Farewell Address, spoke of the "military-industrial complex"—the phrase remembered in a television age—he mentioned other risks that he hoped the nation would give heed to. Expecting the military standoff with the Soviet Union to continue for decades, but knowing war intimately, he spoke of its dangers, emphasizing the imperative need for renewed efforts at arms control. These were matters a military man might be expected to know.

More remarkable, certainly, were Eisenhower's comments on intelligence—not of the covert-spy variety, esteemed at the CIA—but of the kind the nation could never do without. He described America's universities as "the fountainhead of free ideas and scientific discoveries." Lest his words be thought a commonplace presidential tribute to higher education, he added a specific warning, alerting the nation to a new situation created by the Cold War. Knowing the importance of universities and of learning—not in the habit of speaking of a "boutique on the Charles"—he worried lest the universities become the servants of the military. He had no interest in seeing large and very tempting federal grants "substitute for intellectual curiosity." Although his experience as president of Columbia University had been brief, he knew enough from that and from his military/political career to understand the importance of anticipating problems, engaging the public's interest in them.

Such understanding does not exist today, though the President pays almost no political price for his innocence. Still, it is possible that he or those who aspire to be his Republican Party successors will do so soon. When John Maynard Keynes wrote *The Economic Consequences of the Peace,* some admired his courage in mocking Allied war leaders, in seeing them as political peacocks strutting about in the reflected glory of those who had given their lives for a cause he himself deemed dubious. Woodrow Wilson, David Lloyd George, and Georges Clemenceau seemed invincible at the time Keynes wrote, having so recently triumphed in a terrible and costly war. It was taken for granted that they would win the peace as well. Keynes, however, never believed this. Their stars, in fact, began to wane almost immediately after Keynes wrote his tract, but not because of the power of his words. The Allies lost the peace because they scarcely understood the world created by the war of 1914–18. The same destiny awaits America's present leaders, not because of what they did in the Gulf, or failed to do after Saddam's forces were routed, but because they were not able to understand the world they inherited. Ronald Reagan already belongs to the past; George Bush will join him in that oblivion.

Only an American able to mobilize the nation to address its internal problems, to see them for what they are, to understand why their resolution is imperative, can be relied on to lead the country in the new and very dangerous world that is now forming. That world, in any number of respects, replicates that of the United States, with many of the same problems writ large. Only such an individual, respectful of the Constitution, accepting its clear division of responsibilities, can lead the nation out of its present lethargy. No greater opportunity has existed since 1945; none, perhaps, in this century. The Cold War is indeed over, and not only because of what the United States did; a new age is opening, likely to be revolutionary, chaotic, and dangerous. In these circumstances, the society must again be involved, believing in its future, able to imagine it beyond the year 2000. Self-serving myth and fable are useless in a situation that calls for candor and intelligence, for giving new dignity to vision and moral concern.

# Index